MW01610779

KINGDOM THEOLOGY

Three Manifestations & Three Dispensations

of the

Kingdom of Heaven

Dr. Lyle Lee, B. Th., M. Th. S., Dr. Th.

Kingdom Theology

Wordclay

1663 Liberty Drive, Suite 200
Bloomington, IN 47403
www.wordclay.com

First published by Wordclay on 10/2/2008

ISBN: 978-1-6048-1356-2 (sc)

Printed in the United States of America
This book is printed on acid-free paper

Biblical references from:
The Holy Bible, King James Version
(Nashville: Thomas Nelson Inc., 1994)

Table of Contents

Kingdom Theology

Introduction

The Bible has seven dispensations; each dispensation is a time period having a beginning and an ending. Although this is a good general definition of a dispensation, the seventh dispensation has a beginning but does not seem to have an end, rather it continues forever. This study is not about all seven dispensations of the word of God. The last three dispensations of the word of God, deal with the three dispensations of the kingdom of heaven, are the periods we will study concerning *Kingdom Theology*.

There are many names for the kingdom of heaven such as the kingdom of God, or the kingdom of his dear Son, nevertheless all the names refer to the same kingdom of heaven. Only the dispensations and manifestations are different for each kingdom of heaven.

The first dispensation of the kingdom begins at Calvary, and ends at the second coming of Christ. Some theologians call this the church age, or grace period. During this dispensation, the kingdom of heaven is within the heart of all believers. All believers are translated out of the devil's kingdom into the kingdom of Christ. The translation for the believer out of the devil's kingdom happens only to the human spirit. The soul and body are still waiting for salvation, at the second coming of Christ.

During this first dispensation of the kingdom of heaven, the manifestation of this kingdom is seen in the life of the believer. The power of the kingdom is manifested to both the saved and unsaved alike as believers cast out devils, heal the sick, raise the dead, and reveal the Holy Spirit in their lives. The believer gains more understanding of the kingdom of heaven, with the authority and the power, as he studies the word of God and applies the doctrines to his life. The new nature is the ultimate goal for the Christian, as he applies the doctrines of Christ and commandments to his life.

As this kingdom of heaven is ending, three things will take place according to eschatology. The beginning of sorrows, the tribulation being three and one-half years, and the great tribulation being three and one-half years. During these periods, the secret coming of Christ will take place, followed by the rapture of the bride. Then the second coming of Christ will occur, followed by Armageddon. After this, the first resurrection will take place, followed by the rapture of the body of Christ. Then finally, the judgment seat of Christ will close out this dispensation as the millennial kingdom begins.

The next kingdom of heaven starts at the beginning of the millennium and continues for one thousand years. The manifestation of this kingdom of heaven will be physical, and all the governments of the world will become the kingdoms of Christ. During this kingdom of heaven, Satan will be bound for a thousand years in hell along with all the other devils, and peace shall rule the earth. The scriptures inform us that the animals' nature will revert to that of a vegetarian, while the knowledge of God will cover the earth as the waters cover the sea. People will still be marrying and given in marriage during this millennium and death will continue until this last enemy is put under Christ's feet. The saints that will inherit the millennial kingdom of heaven will have glorified bodies and will rule and reign with a rod of iron. Many Christians will remain in heaven during the millennium, having been found unworthy to inherit this kingdom. As this dispensation is ending, Satan is loosed from his prison to deceive the four corners of the earth, Gog and Magog. Fire devours all those who follow the devil as they try to attack the saints in Jerusalem. The kingdom is delivered up to God at this time and no war takes place. Satan, along with those fallen angels and un-regenerated human beings, will enter into the white throne judgment and be cast into a lake of fire.

Then we begin a new heaven and new earth. This final dispensation has a beginning but it does not state in the word that it has any end. During this dispensation, the manifestation of the kingdom of heaven is a city called Jerusalem coming down from the third heaven. This city is also known as the Lamb's bride, and its dimensions are found in Revelation 21. Only those saints who receive glorified bodies will inherit this kingdom of heaven. The Lord Jesus Christ will have a throne in this city, as will the Father. All others outside of the kingdom will need the leaves from the tree of life for the healing of the nations. Many saints who died living a carnal life will not be allowed entrance into this final kingdom of heaven, perhaps for all eternity, while the faithful saints that were glorified will have right to the tree of life, and will go in and out of the city of Jerusalem. Those outside of the kingdom of heaven are all carnal Christians who lived a life of sinful pleasures. Let me therefore reiterate these threee dispensations once again briefly.

The first kingdom of heaven came when the Lord Jesus Christ died on the cross and continues until the second coming of Christ. The second dispensation of the kingdom of heaven is a government resting on the shoulders of the Lord Jesus Christ, this is for a millennium. Finally we enter a new heaven and new earth, although this dispensation has a beginning the Apostle John does not conclude any ending throughout the entire book of Revelation.

The Promise of the Kingdom of Heaven

As we examine the prophesies about the kingdom of heaven, we must understand that the kingdom has three manifestations and three dispensations. We will consider all three manifestations and dispensations a little later in the book. The first scripture is about the kingdom of heaven in all three dispensations and manifestations. As we examine this prophesy spoken by the prophet Nathan to King David, we learn that which was spoken regarding the son of David is all about Jesus Christ. The reason for this conclusion is that the genealogy found in both Matthew and Luke teaches that Joseph and Mary were from the loins of King David. We will see how this prophesy from Nathan unfolds through three different dispensations before it reaches the fulfillment.

2 Samuel 7:12   And when thy days be fulfilled, and thou shalt sleep with thy fathers,

Kingdom Theology

I will set up thy seed after thee, which shall proceed out of thy bowels, and I will establish his kingdom. 13 He shall build an house for my name, and I will stablish the throne of his kingdom for ever.

Although Solomon became the next king from the loins of David to rule over Israel, he was not the one spoken of in this prophesy. The scripture stated two truths about the seed of David who would rule the kingdom. We have the promise of a kingdom without end given to a son of David . Here is where Solomon fails to meet the fulfillment of the prophesy. Therefore, we must look for another son of King David to fulfill this prophesy about the kingdom, one that would prove able to rule the kingdom without end. The New Testament starts with the genealogy of Jesus Christ, calling him the son of David and the son of Abraham. These two genealogy records prove that both Joseph and Mary were from the loins of King David.

Matthew 1:1 *The book of the generation of Jesus Christ, the son of David, the son of Abraham. 2 Abraham begat Isaac; and Isaac begat Jacob; and Jacob begat Judas and his* *brethren; 3 And Judas begat Phares and Zara of Thamar; and Phares begat Esrom; and Esrom begat Aram; 4 And Aram begat Aminadab; and Aminadab begat Naasson; and Naasson begat Salmon; 5 And Salmon begat Booz of Rachab; and Booz begat Obed of Ruth; and Obed begat Jesse; 6 And Jesse begat David the king; and David the king begat Solomon of her that had been the wife of Urias; 7 And Solomon begat Roboam; and Roboam begat Abia; and Abia begat Asa; 8 And Asa begat Josaphat; and Josaphat begat Joram; and Joram begat Ozias; 9 And Ozias begat Joatham; and Joatham begat Achaz; and Achaz begat Ezekias; 10 And Ezekias begat Manasses; and Manasses begat Amon; and Amon begat Josias; 11 And Josias begat Jechonias and his brethren, about the time they were carried away to Babylon: 12 And after they were brought to Babylon, Jechonias begat Salathiel; and Salathiel begat Zorobabel; 13 And Zorobabel begat Abiud; and Abiud begat Eliakim; and Eliakim begat Azor; 14 And Azor begat Sadoc; and Sadoc begat Achim; and Achim begat Eliud; 15 And Eliud begat Eleazar; and Eleazar begat Matthan; and Matthan begat Jacob; 16 And*

Jacob begat Joseph the husband of Mary, of whom was born Jesus, who is called Christ.

In verse 1, the Lord Jesus is referred to as the son of David, the son of Abraham. As we study the rest of the verses of the genealogy record, we see that from Abraham, King David was born. Then in verse 6, David begat Solomon and through his genealogy Joseph was born. Notice in verse 16 the father of Joseph is Jacob, and the term is used that Jacob begat Joseph. This means he was his biological father. This statement could not be made about Joseph and Jesus Christ because he was not his biological father. Rather the statement is made that Joseph was the husband of Mary who gave birth to Jesus Christ. Another genealogy record that sheds light on this truth concerning the heir of King David is found in Luke's gospel.

Luke 3:23 *And Jesus himself began to be about thirty years of age, being (as was supposed) the son of Joseph, which was the son of Heli, 24 Which was the son of Matthat, which was the son of Levi, which was the son of Melchi, which was the son of Janna, which was the son of Joseph, 25 Which was the son* *of Mattathias, which was the son of Amos, which was the son of Naum, which was the son of Esli, which was the son of Nagge, **26** Which was the son of Maath, which was the son of Mattathias, which was the son of Semei, which was the son of Joseph, which was the son of Juda, **27** Which was the son of Joanna, which was the son of Rhesa, which was the son of Zorobabel, which was the son of Salathiel, which was the son of Neri, **28** Which was the son of Melchi, which was the son of Addi, which was the son of Cosam, which was the son of Elmodam, which was the son of Er, **29** Which was the son of Jose, which was the son of Eliezer, which was the son of Jorim, which was the son of Matthat, which was the son of Levi, **30** Which was the son of Simeon, which was the son of Juda, which was the son of Joseph, which was the son of Jonan, which was the son of Eliakim, **31** Which was the son of Melea, which was the son of Menan, which was the son of Mattatha, which was the son of Nathan, which was the son of David, **32** Which was the son of Jesse, which was the son of Obed, which was the son of Booz, which was the son of Salmon, which was the son of Naasson, **33***

*Which was the son of Aminadab, which was the son of Aram, which was the son of Esrom, which was the son of Phares, which was the son of Juda, **34** Which was the son of Jacob, which was the son of Isaac, which was the son of Abraham, which was the son of Thara, which was the son of Nachor,*

Notice in verse 34 we have the name Abraham, and through his genealogy David was born as in Matthew. However, the genealogy changes in verse 31, as the son of David is Nathan. Therefore, through the genealogy of Nathan, David's other son, it states that Heli was born the father of Joseph. Although the father of Joseph is different in Matthew from in Luke, it is not a contradiction. A further study on Joseph reveals that the word begat is only found in Matthew's gospel and not in Luke's gospel. Therefore, we conclude that Jacob was the biological father, while Heli was the father-in-law for he did not beget Joseph. He was Mary's father, not Joseph's father. That is why the scripture calls Heli Joseph's father without mentioning that he begat him.

The importance of these two genealogy records is to reveal that Jesus Christ is the seed of David. For truly through Solomon the son of David, Joseph was born, and through Nathan the son of David, Mary was born. Through these two sons of King David were born the so-called parents of Jesus Christ, giving him the right to the throne of King David. The angel Gabriel, who appeared to Mary, told her this very fact.

Luke 1:31 And, behold, thou shalt conceive in thy womb, and bring forth a son, and shalt call his name JESUS. 32 He shall be great, and shall be called the Son of the Highest: and the Lord God shall give unto him the throne of his father David: 33 And he shall reign over the house of Jacob for ever; and of his kingdom there shall be no end.

The prophesy of the angel Gabriel had the twofold meaning spoken of by Nathan the prophet many years before Jesus was born. Notice the angel stated that Jesus was the son of David, confirming the genealogy of both Matthew and Luke. Furthermore, the angel stated that he would have a kingdom without end, thus fulfilling the twofold prophesy of Nathan to King David. Let us consider this prophesy a little more from the Chronicles record, as it is a little more in-depth.

1 Chronicles 17:11   And it shall come to pass, when thy days be expired that thou must go to be with thy fathers, that I will raise up thy seed after thee, which shall be of thy sons; and I will establish his kingdom. 12 He shall build me an house, and I will stablish his throne for ever. 13 I will be his father, and he shall be my son: and I will not take my mercy away from him, as I took it from him that was before thee: 14 But I will settle him in mine house and in my kingdom for ever: and his throne shall be established for evermore. 15 According to all these words, and according to all this vision, so did Nathan speak unto David.

God spoke through the prophet Nathan stating that the son of David would have an established kingdom. Then he proceeded to state that Jesus Christ would build God a house, thus revealing that Christ would build the church (Matthew 16:18-19). The prophesy also stated that Christ Jesus would have an everlasting throne. Furthermore, God makes mention of Jesus Christ as His son. Then the prophet reaffirms these truths a second time, meaning that the thing is established with God and will happen. A prophet himself, King David also gave us insight into the kingdom of heaven as he prayed openly one day.

1 Chronicles 29:10 Wherefore David blessed the LORD before all the congregation: and David said, Blessed be thou, LORD God of Israel our father, for ever and ever. 11 Thine, O LORD, is the greatness, and the power, and the glory, and the victory, and the majesty: for all that is in the heaven and in the earth is thine; thine is the kingdom, O LORD, and thou art exalted as head above all. 12 Both riches and honour come of thee, and thou reignest over all; and in thine hand is power and might; and in thine hand it is to make great, and to give strength unto all.

Perhaps King David knew that Christ would come from his loins. Notice in David's lifetime he warned Solomon to keep the way of the Lord, or he could lose the kingdom. If David believed Solomon was the heir of the prophesy, he would have to believe his kingdom would be without end. Thus the prophesy of Nathan would not be fulfilled through King Solomon. David himself often wrote Psalms about the kingdom belonging to the Lord, not to his physical son.

Psalm 22:28 *For the kingdom is the LORD'S: and he is the governor among the nations.*

Psalm 45:6 *Thy throne, O God, is for ever and ever: the sceptre of thy kingdom is a right sceptre.*

Psalm 103:19 *The LORD hath prepared his throne in the heavens; and his kingdom ruleth over all.*

Psalm 145:11 *They shall speak of the glory of thy kingdom, and talk of thy power;* **12** *To make known to the sons of men his mighty acts, and the glorious majesty of his kingdom.* **13** *Thy kingdom is an everlasting kingdom, and thy dominion endureth throughout all generations.*

King David gave glory to God through these Psalms, as he magnified the truth about the kingdom of heaven. Another prophet that enlightens us about the kingdom of heaven is the prophet Daniel. After the ten northern tribes went into captivity by Assyria, the last two tribes went into captivity by the Babylonians. Daniel was taken into captivity in the reign of Nebuchadnezzar. The prophet Jeremiah spoke of this captivity to be seventy years long in order for the land to receive her Sabbaths.

It was during this period, while Nebuchadnezzar was reigning, that he dreamed a dream which no man could interpret. Now because no one could interpret the dream, the king had determined to kill all the wise men of Babylon, which included Daniel and his three friends. Then Daniel requested time from the king, and he would make known the dream and its interpretation.

Daniel 2:31 *Thou, O king, sawest, and behold a great image. This great image, whose brightness was excellent, stood before thee; and the form thereof was terrible. 32 This image's head was of fine gold, his breast and his arms of silver, his belly and his thighs of brass, 33 His legs of iron, his feet part of iron and part of clay. 34 Thou sawest till that a stone was cut out without hands, which* *smote the image upon his feet that were of iron and clay, and brake them to pieces.* **35** *Then was the iron, the clay, the brass, the silver, and the gold, broken to pieces together, and became like the chaff of the summer threshingfloors; and the wind carried them away, that no place was found for them: and the stone that smote the image became a great mountain, and filled the whole earth.* **36** *This is the dream; and we will tell the interpretation thereof before the king.* **37** *Thou, O king, art a king of kings: for the God of heaven hath given thee a kingdom, power, and strength, and glory.* **38** *And wheresoever the children of men dwell, the beasts of the field and the fowls of the heaven hath he given into thine hand, and hath made thee ruler over them all. Thou art this head of gold.* **39** *And after thee shall arise another kingdom inferior to thee, and another third kingdom of brass, which shall bear rule over all the earth.* **40** *And the fourth kingdom shall be strong as iron: forasmuch as iron breaketh in pieces and subdueth all things: and as iron that breaketh all these, shall it break in pieces and bruise.* **41** *And whereas thou sawest the feet and toes, part of potters' clay, and part of* *iron, the kingdom shall be divided; but there shall be in it of the strength of the iron, forasmuch as thou sawest the iron mixed with miry clay. **42** And as the toes of the feet were part of iron, and part of clay, so the kingdom shall be partly strong, and partly broken. **43** And whereas thou sawest iron mixed with miry clay, they shall mingle themselves with the seed of men: but they shall not cleave one to another, even as iron is not mixed with clay. **44** And in the days of these kings shall the God of heaven set up a kingdom, which shall never be destroyed: and the kingdom shall not be left to other people, but it shall break in pieces and consume all these kingdoms, and it shall stand for ever. **45** Forasmuch as thou sawest that the stone was cut out of the mountain without hands, and that it brake in pieces the iron, the brass, the clay, the silver, and the gold; the great God hath made known to the king what shall come to pass hereafter: and the dream is certain, and the interpretation thereof sure.*

The king's dream revealed four kingdoms that would rule the world. The fifth kingdom is the kingdom of heaven, in which the Lord Jesus Christ will be the king. This is the stone cut out of the mountain, which destroys the rest of the four kingdoms before it. The first kingdom being revealed here is the Babylonian kingdom; this is the head of gold in verse 38. The second kingdom is the kingdom of the Medes and Persians. They are referred to as the breast and the arms of silver, also called an inferior kingdom in comparison to Babylon (verses 32 & 39). The third kingdom spoken of here is one that Alexander the Great started, which finally became the Roman Empire. They are referred to here as the belly and thighs of brass (verses 32 &39). The fourth kingdom is the anti-Christ kingdom, which has not yet ruled the world, but will during the tribulation period. The fourth kingdom is referred to as the legs of iron, and the feet part of iron and clay (verses 33 & 40-43). Then there was a great mountain in the earth, a reference about the church of Jesus Christ. The stone cut out of this mountain without hands is the foundation or cornerstone Jesus Christ. This kingdom is referred to as having no end, and is a further confirmation of the same kingdom spoken of by Nathan to King David. When the Lord returns he will destroy the anti-Christ kingdom first, then the Roman Empire, then the Medes and Persian, and finally the Babylonian kingdom. This is understood by the stone smiting the feet, until the entire man falls and is destroyed. For when the God of heaven sets up a kingdom (millennial kingdom), he shall break in pieces all these former kingdoms. Notice the wind blows away the dust of these kingdoms, thus revealing the Holy Ghost (wind) will remove all understanding of how to rule the earth with man's knowledge of a kingdom (verses 35 & 44-45). King Nebuchadnezzar exalted Daniel for revealing and interpreting the dream.

Twice recorded in the life of king Nebuchadnezzar, did he openly declare God's eternal kingdom.

Daniel 4:1 *Nebuchadnezzar the king, unto all people, nations, and languages, that dwell in all the earth; Peace be multiplied unto you. 2 I thought it good to shew the signs and wonders that the high God hath wrought toward me. 3 How great are his signs! and how mighty are his wonders! his kingdom is an everlasting kingdom, and his dominion is* *from generation to generation.*

Daniel 4:34 *And at the end of the days I Nebuchadnezzar lifted up mine eyes unto heaven, and mine understanding returned unto me, and I blessed the most High, and I praised and honoured him that liveth for ever, whose dominion is an everlasting dominion, and his kingdom is from generation to generation: 35 And all the inhabitants of the earth are reputed as nothing: and he doeth according to his will in the army of heaven, and among the inhabitants of the earth: and none can stay his hand, or say unto him, What doest thou?*

As we further study the book of Daniel, the prophet is given divine revelation about Jesus Christ and his kingdom. Furthermore, he gives a description of the Father giving the Son the kingdom. Daniel reveals that the kingdom of heaven given to Jesus Christ would rule the entire world. Every nation and language would be under the kingdom of Jesus Christ. This is also a reference about the millennial kingdom, which allows us to know that during the millennium different languages will continue.

Daniel 7:13 I saw in the night visions, and, behold, one like the Son of man came with the clouds of heaven, and came to the Ancient of days, and they brought him near before him. 14 And there was given him dominion, and glory, and a kingdom, that all people, nations, and languages, should serve him: his dominion is an everlasting dominion, which shall not pass away, and his kingdom that which shall not be destroyed.

The prophet Daniel continues to reveal the four kingdoms of men, and the final kingdom of Jesus Christ, which will be eternal. Let us consider for a moment that when the prophet Daniel saw these four kingdoms of men, only the first was a reality. Then the next two kingdoms happened according to the dream God had given Nebuchadnezzar. Therefore the fourth kingdom will also happen, as will the kingdom of heaven given to Jesus Christ. Daniel's description of the four kingdoms of men gives us greater insight into the four kingdoms, more than the dream that Nebuchadnezzar had.

Daniel 7:1   In the first year of Belshazzar

king of Babylon Daniel had a dream and visions of his head upon his bed: then he wrote the dream, and told the sum of the matters. 2 Daniel spake and said, I saw in my vision by night, and, behold, the four winds of the heaven strove upon the great sea. 3 And four great beasts came up from the sea, diverse one from another. 4 The first was like a lion, and had eagle's wings: I beheld till the wings thereof were plucked, and it was lifted up from the earth, and made stand upon the feet as a man, and a man's heart was given to it. 5 And behold another beast, a second, like to a bear, and it raised up itself on one side, and it had three ribs in the mouth of it between the teeth of it: and they said thus unto it, Arise, devour much flesh. 6 After this I beheld, and lo another, like a leopard, which had upon the back of it four wings of a fowl; the beast had also four heads; and dominion was given to it. 7 After this I saw in the night visions, and behold a fourth beast, dreadful and terrible, and strong exceedingly; and it had great iron teeth: it devoured and brake in pieces, and stamped the residue with the feet of it: and it was diverse from all the beasts that were before it; and it had ten horns. 8 I considered the horns, and, behold, there came up among them another little horn, before whom there were three of the first horns plucked up by the roots: and, behold, in this horn were eyes like the eyes of man, and a mouth speaking great things. 9 I beheld till the thrones were cast down, and the Ancient of days did sit, whose garment was white as snow, and the hair of his head like the pure wool: his throne was like the fiery flame, and his wheels as burning fire. 10 A fiery stream issued and came forth from before him: thousand thousands ministered unto him, and ten thousand times ten thousand stood before him: the judgment was set, and the books were opened. 11 I beheld then because of the voice of the great words which the horn spake: I beheld even till the beast was slain, and his body destroyed, and given to the burning flame. 12 As concerning the rest of the beasts, they had their dominion taken away: yet their lives were prolonged for a season and time. 13 I saw in the night visions, and, behold, one like the Son of man came with the clouds of heaven, and came to the Ancient of days, and they brought him near before him. 14 And there was given him dominion, and glory, and a kingdom, that all people, nations, and languages, should serve him: his dominion is an everlasting dominion, which shall not pass away, and his kingdom that which shall not be destroyed. 15 I Daniel was grieved in my spirit in the midst of my body, and the visions of my head troubled me. 16 I came near unto one of them that stood by, and asked him the truth of all this. So he told me, and made me know the interpretation of the things. 17 These great beasts, which are four, are four kings, which shall arise out of the earth. 18 But the saints of the most High shall take the kingdom, and possess the kingdom for ever, even for ever and ever. 19 Then I would know the truth of the fourth beast, which was diverse from all the others, exceeding dreadful, whose teeth were of iron, and his nails of brass; which devoured, brake in pieces, and stamped the residue with his feet; 20 And of the ten horns that were in his head, and of the other which came up, and before whom three fell; even of that horn that had eyes, and a mouth that spake very great things, whose look was more stout than his fellows. 21 I beheld, and the same horn made war with the saints, and prevailed against them; 22 Until the Ancient of days came, and judgment was given to the saints of the most High; and the time came that the saints possessed the kingdom. 23 Thus he said, The fourth beast shall be the fourth kingdom upon earth, which shall be diverse from all kingdoms, and shall devour the whole earth, and shall tread it down, and break it in pieces. 24 And the ten horns out of this kingdom are ten kings that shall arise: and another shall rise after them; and he shall be diverse from the first, and he shall subdue three kings. 25 And he shall speak great words against the most High, and shall wear out the saints of the most High, and think to change times and laws: and they shall be given into his hand until a time and times and the dividing of time. 26 But the judgment shall sit, and they shall take away his dominion, to consume and to destroy it unto the end. 27 And the kingdom and dominion, and the greatness of the kingdom under the whole heaven, shall be given to the people of the saints of the most High, whose kingdom is an everlasting kingdom, and all dominions shall serve and obey him.

In this metaphoric language, we have

knowledge of the four kingdoms of men. The sea in verse 3, which the four beasts came out of, is the different people, nations and languages of the earth. The first kingdom was Babylon, revealed as a lion with eagle's wings in verse 4. The second kingdom is the Medes and Persians; it is the bear, which stood more on one side than the other side. This means that the Persian kingdom was greater than the Medes kingdom when they ruled. This bear had three ribs in its mouth, and devoured much flesh. This speaks of the three kingdoms which the bear destroyed while it reigned over the world (verse 5). The third beast is Alexander the Great, who had four generals under him. According to Matthew Henry's commentary, the four generals and the countries that they ruled over are as follows: Seleucas Nicanor had Asia the Great. Perdiccas, and after him Antigonus, had Asia the Less; Cassander had Macedonia, and Ptolemeus had Egypt. Although these generals divided the world, they did not have a world government. From them came the Roman Empire, which conquered much of the known world, then set up a kingdom. This third beast is the leopard with four wings on its back, and four heads (verse 6). The fourth beast is the anti-Christ kingdom. This beast was dreadful, terrible and very strong, which devoured the previous kingdoms. Perhaps referring to the anti-Christ kingdom as one that will reject the former ways of ruling the world (verse 7). This beast also had ten horns.

We must understand from this verse that Daniel was looking ahead into the future. In the book of Revelation, the apostle John was looking from the future back into history. Therefore, Daniel saw the back of the beast with ten horns, while John saw the front of the beast, with ten horns and seven heads.

Revelation 13:1 *And I stood upon the sand of the sea, and saw a beast rise up out of the sea, having seven heads and ten horns, and upon his horns ten crowns, and upon his heads the name of blasphemy.* *2 And the beast which I saw was like unto a leopard, and his feet were as the feet of a bear, and his mouth as the mouth of a lion: and the dragon gave him his power, and his seat, and great authority.*

Some theologians believe this beast to be

the ten nations from the E.U., and that the seven heads are a representation of the G7. Although the prophet Daniel did not see the seven heads of the beast, both Daniel and John are describing the same beast.

Let us take notice of a few different characteristics from John's view of the beast. This beast comes up out of the sea (sea meaning multitudes of people, nations and languages). The beast looks like a leopard, with bear's feet, and a lion's mouth. All three previous kingdoms are found in this beast; only the order is reversed from Daniel's vision. The leopard is mentioned first here, and not third as in Daniel. That means this beast will have some form of the Roman Empire in it. The bear is mentioned second, as in Daniel. This also means that the anti-Christ kingdom will have some form of the Medes & Persian kingdom in it. In addition, the lion is mentioned third, and not first as in Daniel. This also means that some form of the Babylonian kingdom will also be in the anti-Christ kingdom. Perhaps this will unfold through the religions and philosophy of each kingdom named. In Daniel 7:8, the little horn that comes out from the ten horns is a description of the anti-Christ. One reason he has many eyes is that he will have knowledge of the occult, cults, philosophy, religions, humanism, etc.

In verses 13-14, Daniel saw in visions the Son of man coming to the Ancient of days and receiving a kingdom. His dominion was over the whole world, all nations, and people and languages were under the authority of his kingdom. His kingdom shall never pass away, nor be destroyed. Although these four kingdoms ruled the earth at one time, yet the saints of the Lord shall take possession of the kingdom of heaven forever and ever (verses 17-18). Again, the prophet Daniel had seen the little horn (anti-Christ) think to wear out the saints during the tribulation period. Yet the saints took the kingdom and possessed it forever and ever (verses 19-27). The kingdom of heaven that will begin to rule the earth at the end of the great tribulation is known as the millennial kingdom. The Lord Jesus Christ will be king, sitting upon the throne of David according to the prophesies gone before. Even the angel Gabriel appeared to Mary and told her that the Lord Jesus would sit upon the throne of David, ruling

Israel forever.

Luke 1:26 *And in the sixth month the angel Gabriel was sent from God unto a city of Galilee, named Nazareth, **27** To a virgin espoused to a man whose name was Joseph, of the house of David; and the virgin's name was Mary. **28** And the angel came in unto her, and said, Hail, thou that art highly favoured, the Lord is with thee: blessed art thou among women. **29** And when she saw him, she was troubled at his saying, and cast in her mind what manner of salutation this should be. **30** And the angel said unto her, Fear not, Mary: for thou hast found favour with God. **31** And, behold, thou shalt conceive in thy womb, and bring forth a son, and shalt call his name JESUS. **32** He shall be great, and shall be called the Son of the Highest: and the Lord God shall give unto him the throne of his father David: **33** And he shall reign over the house of Jacob for ever; and of his kingdom there shall be no end.*

The prophesy concerning Jesus Christ receiving a kingdom was fulfilled at his birth. For the angel Gabriel prophesied that Jesus Christ received that kingdom, being heir to the throne of his father David. Although the kingdom was given to Christ Jesus at his birth, the manifestation of that kingdom did not come until his death. Therefore, since Christ Jesus rose from the dead, the promise of King David's son receiving a kingdom without end has now been partially fulfilled.

Hebrews 1:8 *But unto the Son he saith, Thy throne, O God, is for ever and ever: a sceptre of righteousness is the sceptre of thy kingdom.*

The apostle Paul reminds us of this prophesy about the Lord Jesus Christ having a kingdom forever and ever. Here the Father calls the Son "God". Many people struggle with the faith of Jesus being God. Now if the Father believes his Son is God, we as brethren need to believe what the Father believes.

Revelation 1:9 *I John, who also am your brother, and companion in tribulation, and in the kingdom and patience of Jesus Christ, was in the isle that is called Patmos, for the word of God, and for the testimony of Jesus Christ.*

The apostle John is testifying to the fact that the kingdom of heaven is the kingdom of

Christ. His statement about the kingdom and patience of Christ is another testimony to all those who suffer and endure for the kingdom. John considered himself a partaker of the sufferings of Christ, for the kingdom's sake.

Perhaps he was speaking of the kingdom that was present, because he was presently suffering for his faith. Yet this same thought applies to the next kingdom of heaven that the Lord Jesus Christ will bring with him at the second coming. This is better known as the millennial kingdom of heaven. The apostle Paul taught on this kingdom of heaven in many of his epistles to the churches. When he travelled with the apostle Barnabas in the book of Acts, he taught the brethren this truth concerning the millennial kingdom of heaven.

Acts 14:22 Confirming the souls of the disciples, and exhorting them to continue in the faith, and that we must through much tribulation enter into the kingdom of God.

From this verse, it is clear to all believers that we must suffer to enter the millennial kingdom of Christ.

Repent, for the Kingdom of Heaven is Nigh

The first one to preach about the kingdom of heaven was John the Baptist. His message about the kingdom of heaven was bound together with the preaching of repentance. This prophet of God knew that unless people repented of their sins and iniquities, they would neither enter the kingdom of heaven nor see it. When we study the preaching of John, we soon learn he taught all Israel repentance toward God, in preparation for the kingdom of heaven. This prophet of God understood something about the kingdom of heaven that the religious leaders in his day did not understand. The kingdom was nigh, meaning almost present or nearby. This could be better understood as prophesy revealing that the Messiah would have a kingdom in Israel, and the Jews were familiar with these passages. However, John put an urgency upon these truths as though they were about to be fulfilled immediately.

John was born perhaps six months before Jesus Christ, by the cousin of Mary named Elizabeth. He was the son of a Levite named Zachariah, and entitled to the priesthood according to the Mosaic Law. This meant that as a priest, he was allowed to minister in the temple of God. Nevertheless, he was raised in the wilderness until the day of his showing to Israel. John was the first to teach water baptism. His baptism was first introduced to Israel to prepare hearts for the kingdom. One of his main messages was about the kingdom of heaven, and the condition of entering into it.

Matthew 3:1 *In those days came John the Baptist, preaching in the wilderness of Judaea, 2 And saying, Repent ye: for the kingdom of heaven is at hand.*

The understanding to Israel concerning the kingdom of heaven was that the kingdom was nigh at hand. John was not alive when the kingdom of heaven came, but he knew it would soon appear. Therefore, his great desire toward Israel was for them to repent. As a prophet he knew that to be prepared for the kingdom of heaven Israel needed repentance. Although John taught water baptism, his message of repentance was a part of preparing Israel for the kingdom of heaven.

The Lord Jesus came to John one day to be baptized by him, but John desired to be baptized by Jesus. Immediately after Jesus was water baptized to fulfill all righteousness, the Spirit led Jesus into the wilderness. After forty days of fasting in the wilderness, Jesus was tempted by the devil and overcame all the temptations by using the word of God.

Afterwards the Lord Jesus began to gather his disciples. John had openly rebuked Herod as an adulterer for marrying his brother Philip's wife, so Herod had John thrown into prison and later killed.

Around this time, the Lord Jesus was preaching his main message about the kingdom of heaven as John had done. Through his teachings he was preparing the people for the coming of the kingdom.

Matthew 4:17 From that time Jesus began to preach, and to say, Repent: for the kingdom of heaven is at hand.

Once again we find the word to Israel of

repentance, because the kingdom of heaven was about to come. The Lord Jesus knew the kingdom of heaven would come when he died on the cross and rose again, therefore he commanded Israel to repent for the time of his death was nearby. We must also remember that without repentance no one can enter into the kingdom of heaven. This type of repentance that causes someone to enter the kingdom of heaven is explained in John 3:3-5.

Whenever someone believes Jesus is the Christ, the one who died for their sin, they are born again and have repented of unbelief. Although no one could enter the kingdom of heaven before Christ died, the commandment was still to repent for it was at hand.

Mark 1:14 *Now after that John was put in prison, Jesus came into Galilee, preaching the gospel of the kingdom of God,* ***15*** *And saying, The time is fulfilled, and the kingdom of God is at hand: repent ye, and believe the gospel.*

The message that the Lord Jesus preached, was the same message John was already preaching to Israel. The promise of the kingdom of heaven was about to be fulfilled, and Israel needed repentance. Only those who repented would be able to enter the kingdom of heaven. The Lord Jesus taught this truth to Nicodemus, stating that you must be born again to see or to enter the kingdom of heaven. Now we know that no one could be born again as long as Jesus was alive, therefore once he died and was resurrected the kingdom of heaven came.

Notes:_____

_____

_____

_____

_____

_____

_____

_____

_____

_____

_____

_____

_____

_____

_____

_____

Jesus Preached Kingdom Theology

***Matthew 4:23**   And Jesus went about all Galilee, teaching in their synagogues, and preaching the gospel of the kingdom, and healing all manner of sickness and all manner of disease among the people.*

As we read these words, we learn that there is a gospel of the kingdom of heaven and we also learn that preaching of the kingdom of heaven and healing were done together. The Lord Jesus often taught and preached about the kingdom of heaven, and then he healed.

***Matthew 6:25** Therefore I say unto you, Take no thought for your life, what ye shall eat, or what ye shall drink; nor yet for your body, what ye shall put on. Is not the life more than meat, and the body than raiment? **26** Behold the fowls of the air: for they sow not, neither do they reap, nor gather into barns; yet your heavenly Father feedeth them. Are ye not* *much better than they? 27 Which of you by taking thought can add one cubit unto his stature? 28 And why take ye thought for raiment? Consider the lilies of the field, how they grow; they toil not, neither do they spin: 29 And yet I say unto you, That even Solomon in all his glory was not arrayed like one of these. 30 Wherefore, if God so clothe the grass of the field, which to day is, and to morrow is cast into the oven, shall he not much more clothe you, O ye of little faith? 31 Therefore take no thought, saying, What shall we eat? or, What shall we drink? or, Wherewithal shall we be clothed? 32 (For after all these things do the Gentiles seek:) for your heavenly Father knoweth that ye have need of all these things. 33 But seek ye first the kingdom of God, and his righteousness; and all these things shall be added unto you.*

In the teachings of the Lord Jesus, we find a certain strength to trust God for our provision. Therefore, if we can trust God to provide for these natural things of life, we only need to seek the kingdom of God and his righteousness. Once we set our heart on the kingdom of God, all these things will be provided for us. We must learn to begin to see another kingdom made without human hands governing this world. Jesus Christ is the king of the kingdom, and we are citizens in that kingdom (Ephesians 2:19). Furthermore, when we come to this understanding we can seek the kingdom and his righteousness more readily.

Matthew 9:35 And Jesus went about all the cities and villages, teaching in their synagogues, and preaching the gospel of the kingdom, and healing every sickness and every disease among the people.

Wherever the Lord Jesus went, he preached about the gospel of the kingdom. We learn some of those teachings from his parables about the kingdom of heaven. Once we start to study Matthew 5:3-10 and Matthew 13, a greater light will be shed on the subject of the gospel of the kingdom. Again, from these verses we must take note of the healing that was being done while the message of the kingdom was being preached. Once again we are told that there is a gospel of the kingdom, and whenever Christ taught this gospel it appears that he also healed.

Kingdom Theology

Matthew 12:25   And Jesus knew their thoughts, and said unto them, Every kingdom divided against itself is brought to desolation; and every city or house divided against itself shall not stand: 26 And if Satan cast out Satan, he is divided against himself; how shall then his kingdom stand? 27 And if I by Beelzebub cast out devils, by whom do your children cast them out? therefore they shall be your judges. 28 But if I cast out devils by the Spirit of God, then the kingdom of God is come unto you.

Many religious people were present when the Lord Jesus cast out devils. They accused him of being one himself, so he explained how a kingdom operates. Satan cannot cast out Satan, or his kingdom would cease to be. However when the Lord Jesus cast out a devil, he explained that he was of another kingdom known as the kingdom of heaven. Therefore having seen the devil cast out of a person, these religious leaders were told that the kingdom of heaven had come close to them.

Matthew 23:13   But woe unto you, scribes and Pharisees, hypocrites! for ye shut up the kingdom of heaven against men: for ye neither go in yourselves, neither suffer ye them that are entering to go in.

In the Old Testament, the knowledge of the kingdom of heaven was spoken of. The religious leaders had perfect knowledge of those scriptures, which referred to the kingdom of heaven. The Lord Jesus rebuked them because they themselves would not repent and prepare to enter the kingdom. Moreover, the Lord rebuked them because they withstood others who would have had faith in the gospel message but were discouraged to believe because of these religious leaders.

***Mark 9:42** And whosoever shall offend one of these little ones that believe in me, it is better for him that a millstone were hanged about his neck, and he were cast into the sea. **43** And if thy hand offend thee, cut it off: it is better for thee to enter into life maimed, than having two hands to go into hell, into the fire that never shall be quenched: **44** Where their worm dieth not, and the fire is not quenched. **45** And if thy foot offend thee, cut it off: it is better for thee to enter halt into life, than* *having two feet to be cast into hell, into the fire that never shall be quenched: **46** Where their worm dieth not, and the fire is not quenched. **47** And if thine eye offend thee, pluck it out: it is better for thee to enter into the kingdom of God with one eye, than having two eyes to be cast into hell fire:*

These words spoken here by the Lord Jesus have their meaning in metaphors. Some people will go to hell because they would not cut off their hand. This is in reference to the work that they do, their hands work in sinful things to earn a living and because of this, they are commanded to cut off their hand, meaning to quit working in a sinful manner. Yet people do not want to repent, because they know if they accept the gospel message they cannot do their sinful work. The same thing could be said about the foot, the places that sinners go they are not willing to stop going to. Sinners know they cannot accept the gospel and keep going to those sinful places, so some will decide not to 'cut off their foot' in order to be saved. The eye referred to here speaks of our perception or our understanding. Sometimes people will not give up ungodly teachings to receive the truth and be saved. They are not willing to pluck out their eye that they might enter into the kingdom of God. We need to remove all hindrances that we might enter the kingdom of heaven today.

Mark 12:28 And one of the scribes came, and having heard them reasoning together, and perceiving that he had answered them well, asked him, Which is the first commandment of all? 29 And Jesus answered him, The first of all the commandments is, Hear, O Israel; The Lord our God is one Lord: 30 And thou shalt love the Lord thy God with all thy heart, and with all thy soul, and with all thy mind, and with all thy strength: this is the first commandment. 31 And the second is like, namely this, Thou shalt love thy neighbour as thyself. There is none other commandment greater than these. 32 And the scribe said unto him, Well, Master, thou hast said the truth: for there is one God; and there is none other but he: 33 And to love him with all the heart, and with all the understanding, and with all the soul, and with all the strength, and to love his neighbour as himself, is more than all whole burnt offerings and sacrifices. 34 And when Jesus saw that he answered discreetly, he said unto him, Thou art not far from the kingdom of God. And no man after that durst ask him any question.

The scribe that answered the Lord Jesus acknowledged something greater than the Mosaic Law, which demanded sacrifice for atonement. To love God is the first commandment, and to love your neighbor is the second commandment. However, without salvation, one would not be able to do these commandments for it is a commandment to believe on the Lord Jesus Christ. This scribe still lacked that certain knowledge, yet he was told that he was not far from the kingdom of God.

Luke 4:43   And he said unto them, I must preach the kingdom of God to other cities also: for therefore am I sent. 44 And he preached in the synagogues of Galilee.

Notice that the main message of Christ Jesus was to preach about the kingdom of God. This is the same meaning as the kingdom of heaven - there is no difference. Often Christ Jesus would preach in the synagogues from town to town about the kingdom of heaven.

Luke 8:1 And it came to pass afterward, that he went throughout every city and village, preaching and shewing the glad tidings of the kingdom of God: and the twelve were with him,

When the Lord Jesus went from place to place, he revealed the glad tidings of the kingdom of God. The glad tidings are bound up with the Isaiah 61:1-2 message. This message taught that the meek would receive good news, and also that the broken-hearted would be healed. Furthermore, it proclaimed liberty to the captives, and the opening of the prison doors. The Lord Jesus also mentioned the acceptable year of the Lord, which perhaps would be the year that Christ died for our sins.

Luke 9:11 And the people, when they knew it, followed him: and he received them, and spake unto them of the kingdom of God, and healed them that had need of healing.

Once again we see the mixture of the preaching of the kingdom of God with healing. I do not believe that Christ Jesus ever separated these two things, for every time the message of the kingdom was being preached or taught, the Lord also healed.

Luke 11:17 But he, knowing their thoughts, said unto them, Every kingdom divided against itself is brought to desolation; and a house divided against a house falleth. 18 If Satan also be divided against himself, how shall his kingdom stand? because ye say that I cast out devils through Beelzebub. 19 And if I by Beelzebub cast out devils, by whom do your sons cast them out? therefore shall they be your judges. 20 But if I with the finger of God cast out devils, no doubt the kingdom of God is come upon you.

The Lord often came up against opposition from religious leaders. These people condemned him for casting out devils by having a stronger devil in him than the people he helped had in them. This is why the Lord taught about a kingdom being divided - neither can Satan's kingdom be divided nor God's. Satan cannot cast out devils nor can he heal, yet the Lord Jesus did cast out devils to show the people he was of another kingdom. People need to know that whenever a devil is cast out, the kingdom of God is come unto them.

Luke 12:22 *And he said unto his disciples, Therefore I say unto you, Take no thought for your life, what ye shall eat; neither for the body, what ye shall put on. **23** The life is more than meat, and the body is more than raiment. **24** Consider the ravens: for they neither sow nor reap; which neither have storehouse nor barn; and God feedeth them: how much more are ye better than the fowls? **25** And which of you with taking thought can add to his stature one cubit? **26** If ye then be not able to do that thing which is least, why take ye thought for the rest? **27** Consider the lilies how they grow: they toil not, they spin not; and yet I say unto you, that Solomon in all his glory was not arrayed like one of these. **28** If then God so clothe the grass, which is to day in the field, and to morrow is cast into the oven; how much more will he clothe you, O ye of little faith? **29** And seek not ye what ye shall eat, or what ye shall drink, neither be ye of doubtful mind. **30** For all these things do the nations of the world seek after: and your Father knoweth that ye have need of these things. **31** But rather seek ye the kingdom of God; and all these things shall be added unto* *you. 32 Fear not, little flock; for it is your Father's good pleasure to give you the kingdom.*

The main thought here is that if God takes care of the animals which are not eternal, how much more do you think he will take care of man who is eternal? Therefore the commandment to the believer is to set his heart on seeking the kingdom of heaven and then all things will be given to him.

Luke 16:16 *The law and the prophets were until John: since that time the kingdom of God is preached, and every man presseth into it.*

The law spoken of here could be the Mosaic Law, or it could be the Ten Commandments, which is the law of God. The Lord Jesus destroyed the Mosaic Law on the cross (Ephesians 2:14-16 & Colossians 2:14-15), while he magnified the Ten Commandments giving them a spiritual meaning. The kingdom was first preached by John the Baptist. Many believed, were baptized, and through repentance were awaiting the kingdom to come. They were pressing into the kingdom by faith, although the kingdom of heaven did not come until Christ Jesus died on the cross.

Luke 17:20 And when he was demanded of the Pharisees, when the kingdom of God should come, he answered them and said, The kingdom of God cometh not with observation: 21 Neither shall they say, Lo here! or, lo there! for, behold, the kingdom of God is within you.

The Pharisees heard Jesus often teach or preach about the kingdom of God, so they demanded to know when it should come. Their thoughts were on a physical kingdom of heaven because of the prophesies in the Old Testament. They knew that Israel would rule the world through the messiah. They thought they would be in control once again as a nation over the Gentiles. However, the Lord Jesus quickly pointed out that the first manifestation of the kingdom of heaven would not be seen with the natural eye but it would be within the heart of each believer.

John 18:36 Jesus answered, My kingdom is not of this world: if my kingdom were of this world, then would my servants fight, that I should not be delivered to the Jews: but now is my kingdom not from hence.

The Lord Jesus spoke these words to Pilate, a man that knew only of earthly kingdoms. Pilate could find no fault in Jesus for having a kingdom that seemingly meant no threat to Pilate or Rome. Here Jesus gave great insight to the believer that his kingdom was not earthly. For our warfare is not with flesh and blood, and our citizenship is not of this world (Ephesians 2:19).

Matthew 5:3 *Blessed are the poor in spirit: for their's is the kingdom of heaven.*

To understand this term poor in spirit, we must read it from Isaiah 61:1-2, meaning to be meek. The thought here is that when someone empties themselves out of their own desires in life, or does not seek their own will but God's, then this person shall inherit the kingdom of heaven. Notice the kingdom of heaven spoken of here is not a gift like salvation, rather it is something a Christian must inherit by obeying the gospel. For truly to obey the gospel, one must become meek or poor in spirit. Humility needs to rule in the heart of all believers.

Luke 6:20 *And he lifted up his eyes on his disciples, and said, Blessed be ye poor: for your's is the kingdom of God.*

The Lord Jesus was speaking to his disciples here and not to everyone that was present. The promise that they would have the kingdom of God was connected to the understanding that they were disciples of Christ. To be disciples of Christ Jesus, they must put themselves under the discipline of his teachings to govern their lives.

Matthew 5:10 *Blessed are they which are persecuted for righteousness' sake: for theirs is the kingdom of heaven.*

These words of the Lord Jesus are directed toward those who will possess the kingdom. The poor in spirit are the humble, while the persecuted are those suffering for the gospel. The understanding given here is directed toward those believers who try to live a godly life based on the word of God.

Greatest or Least in the Kingdom

Matthew 5:19   Whosoever therefore shall break one of these least commandments, and shall teach men so, he shall be called the least in the kingdom of heaven: but whosoever shall do and teach them, the same shall be called great in the kingdom of heaven. 20 For I say unto you, That except your righteousness shall exceed the righteousness of the scribes and Pharisees, ye shall in no case enter into the kingdom of heaven.

Once someone enters the kingdom of heaven through becoming born again, and then breaks a commandment or teaches others to break the commandments, this person shall be least in the kingdom of heaven. The Lord also taught that if someone wanted to be great in the kingdom of heaven he had to keep the commandments, and teach others to keep the commandments.   This is a lifestyle that someone lives, rather than the thought of someone doing these things once or twice. Therefore if you live a life of denying, or affirm the commandments without living the life of obedience yourself, then you will become the least. Moreover, if you teach others to do the commandments and you yourself are obedient in keeping the commandments as a lifestyle, you will inherit the blessing of becoming the greatest in the kingdom.

Matthew 11:11 Verily I say unto you, Among them that are born of women there hath not risen a greater than John the Baptist: notwithstanding he that is least in the kingdom of heaven is greater than he. 12 And from the days of John the Baptist until now the kingdom of heaven suffereth violence, and the violent take it by force.

Luke 7:28 For I say unto you, Among those that are born of women there is not a greater prophet than John the Baptist: but he that is least in the kingdom of God is greater than he.

The kingdom of heaven was under violence

from the days of John the Baptist. John taught the people of Israel to repent for the kingdom's sake. John the Baptist died before the kingdom of heaven came, and although John the Baptist never entered the kingdom of heaven, he was the greatest prophet to come from a woman. However, we must also understand that anyone who is born again has entered the kingdom of heaven, and is now greater than John the Baptist.

Matthew 18:1 *At the same time came the disciples unto Jesus, saying, Who is the greatest in the kingdom of heaven?* **2** *And Jesus called a little child unto him, and set him in the midst of them,* **3** *And said, Verily I say unto you, Except ye be converted, and become as little children, ye shall not enter into the kingdom of heaven.* **4** *Whosoever therefore shall humble himself as this little child, the same is greatest in the kingdom of heaven.*

These verses have a twofold meaning. The first meaning has to do with being born again. When someone becomes born again, his or her spirit is just like a newborn baby. They are commanded to drink the word of God as if it were milk, so that as a baby they might grow (1 Peter 2:1-2). This is also understood in the teachings of the apostle Paul, who taught that old things are passed away and all things are made new (2 Corinthians 5:17). The second interpretation of the verses has to do with humbling ourselves as little children.

Many illustrations can be thought of to explain this concept. For example, children do not make their own decisions but try to obey their parents' decisions. This illustration concludes with the reasoning that the commandments of God govern my life and not my own reasoning or will. We could also note that a child does not have to provide for itself, but is provided for by the parents. The reasoning behind this illustration tells us that God is Jehovah Jireh, the one who provides for me.

Consider also the interpretation of what the Lord spoke of in Matthew 6:33, about first seeking the kingdom of heaven and his righteousness. Adults will make decisions for themselves, but when we become Christians, Christ desires us to become as children in decision making. One example may be asking the Lord who to marry, or who can your friends be now that you're saved, or who can I go into business with, or where am I allowed to go now that I'm a Christian? Seeking permission from God through prayer or through the word of God is the requirement here. In other words you are no longer an adult to make your own decisions but are becoming childlike before God.

Notes:_____

_____

_____

_____

_____

_____

_____

_____

_____

_____

_____

_____

_____

_____

_____

_____

_____

_____

Prayer for the Kingdom

Matthew 6:9   After this manner therefore pray ye: Our Father which art in heaven, Hallowed be thy name. 10 Thy kingdom come. Thy will be done in earth, as it is in heaven. 11 Give us this day our daily bread. 12 And forgive us our debts, as we forgive our debtors. 13 And lead us not into temptation, but deliver us from evil: For thine is the kingdom, and the power, and the glory, for ever. Amen.

Luke 11:1 And it came to pass, that, as he was praying in a certain place, when he ceased, one of his disciples said unto him, Lord, teach us to pray, as John also taught his disciples. 2 And he said unto them, When ye pray, say, Our Father which art in heaven, Hallowed be thy name. Thy kingdom come. Thy will be done, as in heaven, so in earth. 3 Give us day by day our daily bread. 4 And forgive us our sins; for we also forgive every one that is indebted to us. And lead us not into temptation; but deliver us from evil.

In this prayer of the Lord Jesus, we have the understanding of praying for the kingdom to come. This prayer was a reminder to the disciples that the kingdom had not yet come. The next understanding about the kingdom was that the will of God needs to be done in the earth as it is in heaven. The kingdom of God is in the hearts of believers, as they submit themselves to the doctrines of Christ and manifest that they are in submission to the gospel. Once a believer decides to become a disciple by putting his life under the teachings of Christ, then the king of the kingdom rules in the life of the believer.

One of the clearest expressions of God's will for the believer, is to read the word of God every day. The Lord repeated himself on this matter, saying "give us this day", and "our daily bread". The meaning of bread is the bible, or the word of God. The Lord asks the disciple to pray that he will read his bible every day.

The Lord often taught about the kingdom of heaven in his daily teachings. The disciples after hearing these messages about the kingdom of heaven were then sent out to preach what they had learned. We notice that healing was combined with the preaching of the gospel of the kingdom. The disciples witnessed this kind of ministry from the Lord on a daily basis. Then when the time had come, the Lord sent them out to preach in the same manner. The message of the kingdom of heaven was not only something that they prayed for daily, but it was something they were commanded to preach. Those disciples were still under the Mosaic dispensation, yet were praying for the first manifestation of the kingdom of heaven to come in a prayer that Christ had taught them.

Today, however, Christians are not praying for the first manifestation of the kingdom of heaven to come, for that has already been fulfilled. Rather during this dispensation, all believers should know as they pray this prayer of the Lord, that they are asking God to let the next kingdom come, the millennial kingdom.

During the millennium, disciples will also be taught this same prayer. In that dispensation when they are praying thy kingdom come, it will be the New Jerusalem, city of God, that they will be asking God to send on the earth. This dispensation starts in the new heaven and new earth, as God brings the New Jerusalem from the third heaven down to the earth for all the saints who received glorified bodies to dwell in. Only these saints shall have right to enter the city of God.

Notes:_____

_____

_____

_____

_____

_____

_____

_____

_____

_____

_____

_____

_____

_____

_____

_____

_____

_____

_____

Disciples Preached the Gospel of the Kingdom

Matthew 10:7 And as ye go, preach, saying, The kingdom of heaven is at hand. 8 Heal the sick, cleanse the lepers, raise the dead, cast out devils: freely ye have received, freely give.

The Lord Jesus commanded his disciples to preach the kingdom message. The Lord knew the kingdom of heaven would not come until he died. Jesus sent his disciples out to prepare the hearts of the children of Israel to receive the kingdom of heaven when it would come. Let us also notice they were commanded to heal the sick, cleanse the lepers, raise the dead and cast out devils when preaching kingdom theology.

Luke 9:1 Then he called his twelve disciples together, and gave them power and authority over all devils, and to cure diseases. 2 And he sent them to preach the kingdom of God, and to heal the sick.

Once again we notice the disciples were given power to heal and to cast out devils, as they were commanded to preach the kingdom of God. Healing, casting out devils, and miracles are all part of kingdom theology and whenever we preach about the kingdom we should manifest the power of the kingdom. For us to effectively preach about the kingdom of God we must do so with signs and wonders.

1 Corinthians 4:20 For the kingdom of God is not in word, but in power.

This is the understanding that we need today in our theology, for many preach eloquent messages, but without power. No signs or wonders are being performed after the preaching of the word of God.

Luke 9:59 And he said unto another, Follow me. But he said, Lord, suffer me first to go and bury my father. 60 Jesus said unto him, Let the dead bury their dead: but go thou and preach the kingdom of God.

The understanding of allowing things to

come before the ministry must be weighed out very carefully. The Lord Jesus taught this man it was more important to preach about the kingdom of God than to bury his father. Some theologians believe this man's father was not dead but was probably old and near death. What the man was saying therefore was as soon as Dad dies, I'll go preach. Perhaps there may be some truth to this reasoning; nevertheless, the more important thing to do was to preach about the kingdom of heaven.

Luke 10:1 After these things the Lord appointed other seventy also, and sent them two and two before his face into every city and place, whither he himself would come. 2 Therefore said he unto them, The harvest truly is great, but the labourers are few: pray ye therefore the Lord of the harvest, that he would send forth labourers into his harvest. 3 Go your ways: behold, I send you forth as lambs among wolves. 4 Carry neither purse, nor scrip, nor shoes: and salute no man by the way. 5 And into whatsoever house ye enter, first say, Peace be to this house. 6 And if the son of peace be there, your peace shall rest upon it: if not, it shall turn to you again. 7 And in the same house remain, eating and drinking such things as they give: for the labourer is worthy of his hire. Go not from house to house. 8 And into whatsoever city ye enter, and they receive you, eat such things as are set before you: 9 And heal the sick that are therein, and say unto them, The kingdom of God is come nigh unto you. 10 But into whatsoever city ye enter, and they receive you not, go your ways out into the streets of the same, and say, 11 Even the very dust of your city, which cleaveth on us, we do wipe off against you: notwithstanding be ye sure of this, that the kingdom of God is come nigh unto you.

***Luke 10:17** And the seventy returned again with joy, saying, Lord, even the devils are subject unto us through thy name. 18 And he said unto them, I beheld Satan as lightning fall from heaven. 19 Behold, I give unto you power to tread on serpents and scorpions, and over all the power of the enemy: and nothing shall by any means hurt you. 20 Notwithstanding in this rejoice not, that the spirits are subject unto you; but rather rejoice, because your names are written in* *heaven.*

These seventy disciples that Christ had chosen after the twelve apostles, were sent into the towns and villages without any money or food or clothing. They were commanded to eat whatever was given to them from anyone that would receive them and let them stay in their homes. The next commandments were to heal the sick, cast out devils, and perform miracles. As the seventy returned, they were very excited that devils did come out of people whenever they commanded them to in the name of Jesus Christ.

I believe the Lord Jesus would always preach the gospel of the kingdom first, then do miracles or heal or cast out devils and would immediately inform the people that the kingdom of God had come nigh unto them. The very fact that the healing took place, or that the devil was cast out, or the miracle happened was the evidence that there was authority coming from some other place than that of the town or village.

Mark 16:17 *And these signs shall follow them that believe; In my name shall they cast out* *devils; they shall speak with new tongues; 18 They shall take up serpents; and if they drink any deadly thing, it shall not hurt them; they shall lay hands on the sick, and they shall recover. 19 So then after the Lord had spoken unto them, he was received up into heaven, and sat on the right hand of God. 20 And they went forth, and preached every where, the Lord working with them, and confirming the word with signs following. Amen.*

It is quite evident from all the other verses on the kingdom of heaven that signs were given to convince the hearers about the kingdom of heaven. I believe that these verses are saying the same thing: the gospel of the kingdom of heaven must be preached with evidence. Contrary to what some churches believe or theologians teach today, the will of God has not changed on this subject and therefore these signs are still following disciples today. However, if someone denies these truths, the manifestation of the Spirit of God will not operate in their ministry or life because of their unbelief.

Acts 1:1 *The former treatise have I made, O Theophilus, of all that Jesus began both to do* *and teach, 2 Until the day in which he was taken up, after that he through the Holy Ghost had given commandments unto the apostles whom he had chosen: 3 To whom also he shewed himself alive after his passion by many infallible proofs, being seen of them forty days, and speaking of the things pertaining to the kingdom of God:*

After Christ Jesus rose from the dead, he was seen by his apostles for forty days. The purpose of Christ spending time with those disciples was to speak to them about things pertaining to the kingdom of heaven. Perhaps in the short time the Lord Jesus ministered to his disciples he had not conveyed to them all the knowledge he wanted them to possess about the kingdom of heaven. Therefore when he rose from the dead he spent forty more days instructing them about the kingdom of heaven.

Acts 8:5 Then Philip went down to the city of Samaria, and preached Christ unto them. 6 And the people with one accord gave heed unto those things which Philip spake, hearing and seeing the miracles which he did. 7 For unclean spirits, crying with loud voice, came out of many that were possessed with them: and many taken with palsies, and that were lame, were healed. 8 And there was great joy in that city. 9 But there was a certain man, called Simon, which beforetime in the same city used sorcery, and bewitched the people of Samaria, giving out that himself was some great one: 10 To whom they all gave heed, from the least to the greatest, saying, This man is the great power of God. 11 And to him they had regard, because that of long time he had bewitched them with sorceries. 12 But when they believed Philip preaching the things concerning the kingdom of God, and the name of Jesus Christ, they were baptized, both men and women.

When Philip went down into Samaria, the hearts of the people were already prepared to receive more about the gospel of the kingdom of God. Christ had spent some time there with the disciples, teaching them about the kingdom of God (John 4). While Philip preached the gospel to these people, miracles and healings were manifest as they heard about the kingdom of God.

This is the only evangelist named in the New Testament after Christ was raised from the dead. Notice the manner in which he preached the gospel of the kingdom. It was not with words only, but also with signs and wonders.

Another important message from these verses, which needs to be considered, is that this man was not an apostle but an evangelist. The reason we cannot overemphasize this truth is that people today think only the apostles preached with signs following. On the contrary, the scriptures give more reference to those who taught the gospel with signs following who were not apostles, like Silas who travelled with Paul. Also we have previously mentioned the seventy men that Jesus chose to preach with signs following in Luke 10.

Acts 19:1 And it came to pass, that, while Apollos was at Corinth, Paul having passed through the upper coasts came to Ephesus: and finding certain disciples, 2 He said unto them, Have ye received the Holy Ghost since ye believed? And they said unto him, We have not so much as heard whether there be any Holy Ghost. 3 And he said unto them, Unto what then were ye baptized? And they said, Unto John's baptism. 4 Then said Paul, John verily baptized with the baptism of repentance, saying unto the people, that they should believe on him which should come after him, that is, on Christ Jesus. 5 When they heard this, they were baptized in the name of the Lord Jesus. 6 And when Paul had laid his hands upon them, the Holy Ghost came on them; and they spake with tongues, and prophesied. 7 And all the men were about twelve. 8 And he went into the synagogue, and spake boldly for the space of three months, disputing and persuading the things concerning the kingdom of God.

The apostle Paul journeyed to Ephesus where he baptized about twelve disciples of John in water and in the Holy Ghost. Later Paul spent three months in the synagogue arguing and disputing with the Jews about the things that pertained to the kingdom of God. Most Old Testament references about the kingdom of God spoke only about the millennial kingdom. Perhaps Paul had to dispute concerning the kingdom that was now present after the death of Jesus Christ, and prove to these men a different manifestation and dispensation of the kingdom of heaven.

Acts 20:16 For Paul had determined to sail by Ephesus, because he would not spend the time in Asia: for he hasted, if it were possible for him, to be at Jerusalem the day of Pentecost. 17 And from Miletus he sent to Ephesus, and called the elders of the church. 18 And when they were come to him, he said unto them, Ye know, from the first day that I came into Asia, after what manner I have been with you at all seasons, 19 Serving the Lord with all humility of mind, and with many tears, and temptations, which befell me by the lying in wait of the Jews: 20 And how I kept back nothing that was profitable unto you, but have shewed you, and have taught you publickly, and from house to house, 21 Testifying both to the Jews, and also to the Greeks, repentance toward God, and faith toward our Lord Jesus Christ. 22 And now, behold, I go bound in the spirit unto Jerusalem, not knowing the things that shall befall me there: 23 Save that the Holy Ghost witnesseth in every city, saying that bonds and afflictions abide me. 24 But none of these things move me, neither count I my life dear unto myself, so that I might finish my course with joy, and the ministry, which I have received of the Lord Jesus, to testify the gospel of the grace of God. 25 And now, behold, I know that ye all, among whom I have gone preaching the kingdom of God, shall see my face no more. 26 Wherefore I take you to record this day, that I am pure from the blood of all men. 27 For I have not shunned to declare unto you all the counsel of God.

The city of Miletus was close enough for Paul to send for the elders from Ephesus also. Once they were all present, he expounded to them all things concerning his ministry, how he had worked and suffered for the sake of the gospel. He taught all people repentance toward God, and faith in the Lord Jesus Christ. Paul proclaimed clearly that he preached the message of the kingdom of God, as though it was the most important doctrine that he taught.

Acts 28:17 And it came to pass, that after three days Paul called the chief of the Jews together: and when they were come together, he said unto them, Men and brethren, though I have committed nothing against the people, or customs of our fathers, yet was I delivered prisoner from Jerusalem into the hands of the Romans. 18 Who, when they had examined me, would have let me go, because there was no cause of death in me. 19 But when the Jews spake against it, I was constrained to appeal unto Caesar; not that I had ought to accuse my nation of. 20 For this cause therefore have I called for you, to see you, and to speak with you: because that for the hope of Israel I am bound with this chain. 21 And they said unto him, We neither received letters out of Judaea concerning thee, neither any of the brethren that came shewed or spake any harm of thee. 22 But we desire to hear of thee what thou thinkest: for as concerning this sect, we know that every where it is spoken against. 23 And when they had appointed him a day, there came many to him into his lodging; to whom he expounded and testified the kingdom of God, persuading them concerning Jesus, both out of the law of Moses, and out of the prophets, from morning till evening. 24 And some believed the things which were spoken, and some believed not. 25 And when they agreed not among themselves, they departed, after that Paul had spoken one word, Well spake the Holy Ghost by Esaias the prophet unto our fathers, 26 Saying, Go unto this people, and say, Hearing ye shall hear, and shall not understand; and seeing ye shall see, and not perceive: 27 For the heart of this people is waxed gross, and their ears are dull of hearing, and their eyes have they closed; lest they should see with their eyes, and hear with their ears, and understand with their heart, and should be converted, and I should heal them. 28 Be it known therefore unto you, that the salvation of God is sent unto the Gentiles, and that they will hear it. 29 And when he had said these words, the Jews departed, and had great reasoning among themselves. 30 And Paul dwelt two whole years in his own hired house, and received all that came in unto him, 31 Preaching the kingdom of God, and teaching those things which concern the Lord Jesus Christ, with all confidence, no man forbidding him.

After Paul was taken prisoner, Festus desired to take him back to Jerusalem where the Jews wanted to kill him, so Paul appealed to Caesar. For this reason Paul was sent to Rome. Once he was established in his own house, he called the Jewish elders of the city together and explained to them the things concerning the kingdom of God. Then the word tells us he spent two full years in his own house preaching to them about the kingdom.

***Romans 14:17** For the kingdom of God is not meat and drink; but righteousness, and peace, and joy in the Holy Ghost.*

The Mosaic Law forbids the Jewish people certain foods. Christianity, however, is not under the Mosaic Law but is under grace. For this reason, the apostle Paul informs us that as believers we should not give heed to these foolish teachings about meat such as pork, as though it can make us unclean. The scripture teaches that all meats are clean to eat and nothing is to be refused. Once we pray over it, the meat is sanctified (1 Timothy 4:1-5).

The kingdom of God is found in righteousness, meaning obedience to the gospel. Moreover it is found in the peace of the Holy Ghost and the joy of the Holy Ghost, which is the inheritance of all believers concerning the kingdom of God.

1 Corinthians 4:18 Now some are puffed up, as though I would not come to you. 19 But I will come to you shortly, if the Lord will, and will know, not the speech of them which are puffed up, but the power. 20 For the kingdom of God is not in word, but in power.

It would appear from these verses that some of the elders, meaning preachers in the church at Corinth, thought they were better preachers than some of the other ministers. They thought they had better knowledge of the word of God than the next man. The apostle Paul reminds them that the preaching of the kingdom of God is not done with words only, but it is also done with demonstration, meaning to preach with power, cast out devils, heal the sick, raise the dead and cleanse the lepers. This is also how we are to preach the kingdom of God today, not in words only.

Colossians 4:11 And Jesus, which is called Justus, who are of the circumcision. These only are my fellow workers unto the kingdom of God, which have been a comfort unto me.

One of the disciples had the same name as

the Lord, so his name was changed to Justus. This man was a fellow worker of the apostle Paul who probably travelled and suffered with Paul as he preached about the kingdom of God.

As we study the ministry of the disciples, we learn that they were commanded to preach the gospel of the kingdom. The power of God was present to heal, cast out devils, do miracles, raise the dead and cleanse the lepers as they preached.

One of the commandments was to take no money from the unsaved while they preached to them about the kingdom (Matthew 10:7-8 & Luke 9:1-2).

The Lord also appointed seventy more disciples to preach the gospel of the kingdom. They soon learned that there was authority in the name of Jesus Christ. Through his name, they cast out devils and laid hands on the sick, who recovered. The authority was given to these disciples through the name of Jesus Christ (Luke 10:17-20 & Mark 16:17-20). The gospel of the kingdom of heaven was preached and taught by all the disciples, with signs and wonders in the name of the Lord Jesus Christ.

Kingdom Theology

One very important revelation for the church of Jesus Christ during this dispensation is that these things were done in the name of the Lord at the beginning of this dispensation. This does not mean the gospel should no longer be preached this way in our day. On the contrary, this means that during this complete dispensation, until Christ returns, we are commanded to preach the same way in which the earlier disciples preached.

Notes:_____

_____

_____

_____

_____

_____

_____

_____

_____

_____

_____

_____

_____

Manifestations & Dispensations of the Kingdom

The word manifestation means an outward appearance of what we can see with our natural eye. The word dispensation is interpreted as a period with a beginning and an ending. The manifestation and the dispensation of the kingdom of heaven is threefold.

The first manifestation of the kingdom is inwardly, while the dispensation is 2,000 years. Many theologians also speak of this as the church age. During the first manifestation of the kingdom of heaven, believers are given authority and power to witness for the kingdom of heaven which is present (1 Corinthians 4:20). Many times the Lord Jesus calls the church the kingdom of heaven in his parables. Although the manifestation of the kingdom of heaven is within the believer, the outward appearance is seen in the change of the character of the believer. Once a believer overcomes the lust of the eyes, flesh and pride of life, he is manifesting the power and authority of the kingdom of heaven in his life.

Furthermore, whenever a believer heals, casts out devils, speaks in tongues, cleanses a leper or raises the dead, it is an outward appearance of the kingdom of heaven. The first kingdom of heaven is seen when believers manifest its authority and power. In this first manifestation of the kingdom of heaven, the Lord Jesus gives to the church the keys of the kingdom to bind or loose on earth and in heaven (Matthew 16:18-19). The first dispensation began when Christ died on the cross and ends when he returns with the next kingdom. The parables of the kingdom of heaven explain this period more readily, and express the beginning and ending of the first dispensation.

The second manifestation of the kingdom of heaven is a government which will rule the whole world, while the dispensation is for one thousand years. When the Lord Jesus comes the second time to set up his kingdom, all the kingdoms of the world will become the kingdoms of Christ. Again, this second dispensation is for one thousand years, which is commonly called the millennial kingdom or the millennium (Revelation 20:4).

The third manifestation of the kingdom of God is a city which is presently in the third heaven. The length and breadth of the city is found in Revelation 21. This city is also known as the New Jerusalem and the dispensation for this city begins when the millennium ends.

We cannot find any scripture to indicate when this dispensation ends, however. It appears that in the new heaven and the new earth, the kingdom of heaven will have no end. Thus it will fulfill the prophesy about Jesus Christ as the son of David ruling on the throne of David and having a kingdom without end (2 Samuel 7:12-13).

As we survey the scriptures, we will try to place each kingdom and dispensation in chronological order. First we will study the manifestation of the kingdom of God, and then we will study the dispensation of the kingdom. The names kingdom of God, or kingdom of heaven, or kingdom of Christ, or kingdom of his dear Son refer to all three manifestations and dispensations of the one same kingdom. In other words by using the phrase kingdom of heaven we donnot mean a different kingdom than the kingdom of God or the kingdom of his dear Son. All of these difinitions are used by either the Lord Jesus Christ or the Apostle Paul to refer unto this one kingdom which eventually manifests in three different appearances during these three dispensations starting from the death of our Lord Jesus Christ.

Notes:_____

_____

_____

_____

_____

_____

_____

_____

_____

_____

_____

_____

First Manifestation of the Kingdom of Heaven

John 3:3 *Jesus answered and said unto him, Verily, verily, I say unto thee, Except a man be born again, he cannot see the kingdom of God. 4 Nicodemus saith unto him, How can a man be born when he is old? can he enter the second time into his mother's womb, and be born? 5 Jesus answered, Verily, verily, I say unto thee, Except a man be born of water and of the Spirit, he cannot enter into the kingdom of God.*

The beginning of the kingdom is explained to Nicodemus in these few words. The Lord Jesus taught that no one could see or enter the kingdom of heaven unless he was born again. Therefore, the kingdom of heaven would begin when it became possible to be born again. This is why we teach that the kingdom of heaven started from Calvary. After Jesus Christ died on the cross for our sin we could become born again. This correlates with John 3:14-15. From the point of the cross, believers who accepted Christ as sacrifice for their sin would be born again. The apostle Paul writes that if we confess the Lord Jesus and believe God raised him from the dead, we will be saved (Romans 10:9). Paul also includes the resurrection, with the death and burial of Christ, as giving salvation. This correlates with John 3:16. There are however many other scriptures from the apostle Paul indicating that redemption was from the blood, and so was sanctification from the body of Christ at Calvary (Ephesians 1:7 & Hebrews 10:10).

The Lord Jesus taught that when someone is saved, or born again, he enters the kingdom of heaven. This is the manifestation of the kingdom of God in the believer's life, which is clearly seen by others as the disciple grows in the knowledge of the most high. The Lord Jesus taught that once a person is born again, he will begin to see the kingdom of God in his life as a change in his nature or his character. Furthermore, the believer will start to understand the power and the authority of the kingdom of heaven in his personal life. The outward manifestation of the kingdom of heaven operating in the believer's life will be seen by the unsaved. This is what is meant by seeing the kingdom of heaven in John 3:3. The word see in this verse is used to mean perception or understanding. Once a believer enters the kingdom of heaven he begins to perceive the laws, power and authority of the kingdom of God. The laws are explained as sowing and reaping, and the believer begins to understand these precepts even more as he practices them. Before the Lord Jesus died, he told his disciples that some of them would not die until they had personally seen the kingdom of God.

Mark 9:1 And he said unto them, Verily I say unto you, That there be some of them that stand here, which shall not taste of death, till they have seen the kingdom of God come with power.

Christ Jesus taught his disciples that they would see the kingdom come with power, meaning the Holy Ghost. Judas Iscariot would not be among those who would see the kingdom coming with power, as he committed suicide before the kingdom came.

This prophesy to those disciples had to be fulfilled before they died, which would mean that the kingdom of God had to come while they were alive. We must conclude one of three things: either the kingdom of God has come already, or those disciples are still alive, or the prophesy was false.

This prophesy of Christ spoke to the disciples needs careful consideration. If this is a true prophesy, then the kingdom of God is present today.

In fact, the outward manifestation of the kingdom of God coming with power was fulfilled on the day of Pentecost, as 120 disciples waited in the upper room in obedience to what the Lord said to them after he rose from the dead. He commanded his disciples to wait for the promise of the father, which was the Holy Ghost (Luke 24:46-49).

Acts 2:1 And when the day of Pentecost was fully come, they were all with one accord in one place. 2 And suddenly there came a sound from heaven as of a rushing mighty wind, and it filled all the house where they were sitting. 3 And there appeared unto them cloven tongues like as of fire, and it sat upon *each of them. **4** And they were all filled with the Holy Ghost, and began to speak with other tongues, as the Spirit gave them utterance.*

While the disciples waited for the promise of the father, the Holy Ghost was sent to them on the day of Pentecost. All 120 disciples were filled with the Holy Ghost, fulfilling the prophesy concerning the kingdom of God coming with power. The Lord told them some of them would not die until they had seen the kingdom of God coming in power, and on the day of Pentecost, this was fulfilled. Although we must make mention that the kingdom of heaven came when Jesus Christ died on the cross, yet the power was received on the day of Pentecost.

Once the kingdom of God had come with power, the establishing of the kingdom was the priority. The fact that the Lord Jesus Christ would rule this kingdom was already prophesied to King David through Nathan many years before (2 Samuel 7:12-13). This is what the angel Gabriel told Mary when he informed her of Christ coming into the world through her.

Luke 1:26 And in the sixth month the angel Gabriel was sent from God unto a city of Galilee, named Nazareth, 27 To a virgin espoused to a man whose name was Joseph, of the house of David; and the virgin's name was Mary. 28 And the angel came in unto her, and said, Hail, thou that art highly favoured, the Lord is with thee: blessed art thou among women. 29 And when she saw him, she was troubled at his saying, and cast in her mind what manner of salutation this should be. 30 And the angel said unto her, Fear not, Mary: for thou hast found favour with God. 31 And, behold, thou shalt conceive in thy womb, and bring forth a son, and shalt call his name JESUS. 32 He shall be great, and shall be called the Son of the Highest: and the Lord God shall give unto him the throne of his father David: 33 And he shall reign over the house of Jacob for ever; and of his kingdom there shall be no end.

The angel Gabriel told Mary that her son would be the Son of God. Furthermore, he would sit on the throne of David and rule all Israel for eternity. This prophesy spoken to David by Nathan the prophet was partially being fulfilled here concerning Jesus Christ.

Kingdom Theology

Although at his birth we do not see him ruling over all Israel, nevertheless he was the king of the kingdom from birth and the fulfillment of the prophesy to King David in 2 Samuel 7:12-13.

The fact that Jesus was ruling Israel is seen in his authority over devils and sicknesses that plagued Israel, and more explicitly over the Jewish disciples. Nevertheless, more than once the Lord proclaimed his kingdom was not of this world, which was a reference concerning the outward manifestation of his kingdom. Yet his kingdom, in which he alone is king, was taught in all his parables about the kingdom. Therefore we can affirm that the kingdom of heaven dwells within the heart of the believer and is not seen with the natural eye (Luke 17:20-2). It is seen in power and demonstration by those disciples which believe and practice the scriptures dealing with the outward manifestation of the kingdom of heaven (e.g. Mark 16:17-19, Matthew 10:7-8, Mark 16:17-18, Luke 10:17). Moreover, it is fruit borne by those disciples which practice the manifestation of the kingdom of God, by the power and authority of the kingdom while they preach (1

Corinthians 4:20). Whenever a miracle is done in the name of Jesus Christ, the proclamation that Christ has all authority in heaven and in earth is made openly. Whenever a healing is done in the name of the Lord, the disciple is manifesting the authority of the King of Israel to the unsaved and saved alike. Moreover, it is a witness that Christ rose from the dead and is seated at the right hand of the father, having all power and authority (Matthew 28:18-20).

Christ often spoke of kingdom theology. Many religious leaders of the day who knew something about the kingdom, would approach Christ on this subject.

Luke 17:20 And when he was demanded of the Pharisees, when the kingdom of God should come, he answered them and said, The kingdom of God cometh not with observation: 21 Neither shall they say, Lo here! or, lo there! for, behold, the kingdom of God is within you.

The Pharisees did not know about kingdom theology, although they did understand something about the kingdom from the prophets and Psalms. The only understanding they had about the kingdom was that it would be a physical kingdom that would rule the world. It appears that they knew about the millennial kingdom but had no knowledge of the kingdom of heaven within the believer. Consequently, they wanted to know when the kingdom would come, for they believed in the kingdom of Israel. Their belief was about a physical kingdom, not a spiritual one.

Whenever the Lord Jesus taught on the kingdom of heaven, he would mostly use parables describing the kingdom. However, when he was alone with his disciples, they would ask him to interpret those parables, which he proclaimed openly. As we study the parables on the kingdom of heaven, we will try to put them in a kind of chronological order. These will be the parables about the first manifestation of the kingdom of heaven, then the millennial manifestation and dispensation of the kingdom of heaven.

Matthew 13:1 The same day went Jesus out of the house, and sat by the sea side. 2 And great multitudes were gathered together unto him, so that he went into a ship, and sat; and the whole multitude stood on the shore. 3 And he spake many things unto them in parables, saying, Behold, a sower went forth to sow; 4 And when he sowed, some seeds fell by the way side, and the fowls came and devoured them up: 5 Some fell upon stony places, where they had not much earth: and forthwith they sprung up, because they had no deepness of earth: 6 And when the sun was up, they were scorched; and because they had no root, they withered away. 7 And some fell among thorns; and the thorns sprung up, and choked them: 8 But other fell into good ground, and brought forth fruit, some an hundredfold, some sixtyfold, some thirtyfold. 9 Who hath ears to hear, let him hear. 10 And the disciples came, and said unto him, Why speakest thou unto them in parables? 11 He answered and said unto them, Because it is given unto you to know the mysteries of the kingdom of heaven, but to them it is not given.

***Matthew 13:18** Hear ye therefore the parable of the sower. 19 When any one heareth the word of the kingdom, and understandeth it not, then cometh the wicked one, and catcheth away that which was sown in his heart. This is he which received seed by the way side. 20 But he that received the seed into stony* *places, the same is he that heareth the word, and anon with joy receiveth it; 21 Yet hath he not root in himself, but dureth for a while: for when tribulation or persecution ariseth because of the word, by and by he is offended. 22 He also that received seed among the thorns is he that heareth the word; and the care of this world, and the deceitfulness of riches, choke the word, and he becometh unfruitful. 23 But he that received seed into the good ground is he that heareth the word, and understandeth it; which also beareth fruit, and bringeth forth, some an hundredfold, some sixty, some thirty.*

Mark 4:1 And he began again to teach by the sea side: and there was gathered unto him a great multitude, so that he entered into a ship, and sat in the sea; and the whole multitude was by the sea on the land. 2 And he taught them many things by parables, and said unto them in his doctrine, 3 Hearken; Behold, there went out a sower to sow: 4 And it came to pass, as he sowed, some fell by the way side, and the fowls of the air came and devoured it up. 5 And some fell on stony ground, where it had not much earth; and immediately it sprang up, because it had no depth of earth: 6 But when the sun was up, it was scorched; and because it had no root, it withered away. 7 And some fell among thorns, and the thorns grew up, and choked it, and it yielded no fruit. 8 And other fell on good ground, and did yield fruit that sprang up and increased; and brought forth, some thirty, and some sixty, and some an hundred. 9 And he said unto them, He that hath ears to hear, let him hear. 10 And when he was alone, they that were about him with the twelve asked of him the parable. 11 And he said unto them, Unto you it is given to know the mystery of the kingdom of God: but unto them that are without, all these things are done in parables:

Mark 4:14 *The sower soweth the word. 15 And these are they by the way side, where the word is sown; but when they have heard, Satan cometh immediately, and taketh away the word that was sown in their hearts. 16 And these are they likewise which are sown on stony ground; who, when they have heard the word, immediately receive it with gladness; 17 And have no root in themselves, and so endure but for a time: afterward, when affliction or persecution ariseth for the*

word's sake, immediately they are offended.
***18** And these are they which are sown among
thorns; such as hear the word,* ***19** And the
cares of this world, and the deceitfulness of
riches, and the lusts of other things entering
in, choke the word, and it becometh unfruitful.*
***20** And these are they which are sown on
good ground; such as hear the word, and
receive it, and bring forth fruit, some
thirtyfold, some sixty, and some an hundred.*

***Luke 8:5** A sower went out to sow his seed:
and as he sowed, some fell by the way side;
and it was trodden down, and the fowls of the
air devoured it.* ***6** And some fell upon a rock;
and as soon as it was sprung up, it withered
away, because it lacked moisture.* ***7** And some
fell among thorns; and the thorns sprang up
with it, and choked it.* ***8** And other fell on
good ground, and sprang up, and bare fruit
an hundredfold. And when he had said these
things, he cried, He that hath ears to hear, let
him hear.* ***9** And his disciples asked him,
saying, What might this parable be?* ***10** And
he said, Unto you it is given to know the
mysteries of the kingdom of God: but to
others in parables; that seeing they might not
see, and hearing they might not understand.*

11 Now the parable is this: The seed is the word of God. 12 Those by the way side are they that hear; then cometh the devil, and taketh away the word out of their hearts, lest they should believe and be saved. 13 They on the rock are they, which, when they hear, receive the word with joy; and these have no root, which for a while believe, and in time of temptation fall away. 14 And that which fell among thorns are they, which, when they have heard, go forth, and are choked with cares and riches and pleasures of this life, and bring no fruit to perfection. 15 But that on the good ground are they, which in an honest and good heart, having heard the word, keep it, and bring forth fruit with patience.

In this parable of the sower and the seed, the Lord explains the first manifestation of the kingdom of heaven. The sowers are those preaching the word of God, who go throughout the world preaching the gospel. The seed is the word of God which is sown in the hearts of mankind. All those who receive Jesus Christ as Lord have entered the kingdom of heaven, meaning the church. We will learn from the parables that the kingdom of heaven is in reference to either the church, or Christ himself. The Lord then explains the four kinds of hearts that are in the kingdom of God.

The first heart is the people who become born again, but have the word stolen from them by the devil so they never produce any fruit for God by obeying the gospel. Although they believe Jesus Christ died for their sins, their hearts are hard because they have never repented of their sins. They have only turned from unbelief concerning Christ as Messiah, to believing he is the Lamb of God that takes away the sin of the world.

The second heart spoken of here is the people who are born again but still have some unrepented sins. Although they probably dealt with some bigger sins in their life, and repented of them, still other sins are not yet repented of. Therefore a bed of stones lies in their hearts, stopping the word from going in deeper to cause a greater change in character.

The third heart in the kingdom is those who have repented of their sins but want to live for self-indulgence. They desire riches, fame, and the glory of mankind. Some of these believers (including preachers) who actually think or teach that to be godly leads to riches, thus think godliness is gain. The apostle Paul tells us to avoid these believers, and taught that they are fruitless (1 Timothy 6: 5).

The fourth heart in the parable of the sower is the born-again believers who obey the gospel. First they have repented of their sins, breaking up the fallow ground of their hearts in order for the seed to go down deep into the heart and produce fruit. In addition, they have removed all the stones (sins) which would stop the seed from growing deep roots. These good-ground believers have not allowed thorns to grow in the ground and do not seek riches or glory. The fourth heart of good ground is the believers who produces fruit, to varying degrees.

Mark 4:26 And he said, So is the kingdom of God, as if a man should cast seed into the ground; 27 And should sleep, and rise night and day, and the seed should spring and grow up, he knoweth not how. 28 For the earth bringeth forth fruit of herself; first the blade, then the ear, after that the full corn in the ear. 29 But when the fruit is brought forth, immediately he putteth in the sickle, because the harvest is come.

This parable about the church of Jesus Christ explains how the church came into existence. The man that sowed the seed is God the father, and the seed is Jesus Christ. The Lord Jesus goes into the earth and dies, bringing forth the church in the infant stages. Afterward, the church goes on to becoming more fully grown until finally it reaches the harvest. This is the growth of the church, until the Lord Jesus returns to rapture his bride.

Matthew 13:31 *Another parable put he forth unto them, saying, The kingdom of heaven is like to a grain of mustard seed, which a man took, and sowed in his field: **32** Which indeed is the least of all seeds: but when it is grown, it is the greatest among herbs, and becometh a tree, so that the birds of the air come and lodge in the branches thereof.*

Mark 4:30 *And he said, Whereunto shall we liken the kingdom of God? or with what comparison shall we compare it? **31** It is like a grain of mustard seed, which, when it is sown in the earth, is less than all the seeds* *that be in the earth: **32** But when it is sown, it groweth up, and becometh greater than all herbs, and shooteth out great branches; so that the fowls of the air may lodge under the shadow of it.*

***Luke 13:18** Then said he, Unto what is the kingdom of God like? and whereunto shall I resemble it? **19** It is like a grain of mustard seed, which a man took, and cast into his garden; and it grew, and waxed a great tree; and the fowls of the air lodged in the branches of it.*

In this parable, the kingdom of heaven is likened unto Jesus Christ, and the church of Jesus Christ. Christ is both the seed of Abraham and the seed of David. The word 'seed' in these texts refer to Christ Jesus as having a human body (Hebrews 2:16). The mustard seed in this parable is the Lord Jesus Christ himself. He is the seed taken and sown into the world through his death and burial. The man that sowed him is God the father, thus fulfilling the scriptures, like Isaiah 53. Once Christ dies, he produces the greatest tree in the earth, the mustard tree. This is the explanation of how the church came into being. Through the death of the mustard seed, the mustard tree grew. Unless a seed goes into the ground and dies, it abides alone.

The thought of the church being a mustard tree is very significant and explains that the church would suffer more than any others. The mustard herb may be very bitter or hot. My personal conclusion about this illustration of the mustard tree is like the gospel of Paul, who said we are not only to believe on the Lord Jesus Christ but are also commanded to suffer also for his sake (Philippians 1:29). The prophetic truth about this parable rings out profoundly today, as we look a little deeper into the birds lodged in the branches of this tree. Once the church grows (mustard tree), the devils are sometimes in the pulpits and pews of the church (birds lodged in the branches). The Lord Jesus taught in the parable of the sower that the birds were devils (Matthew 13:3-4 & 19). This is why we have so many different cults springing up calling themselves Christian. The apostle Paul taught that in the last days, the church of Jesus Christ would have seducing spirits and devil doctrine in it. For this reason, some would leave the doctrine of the Lord Jesus Christ (1

Timothy 4).

A revelation of this particular parable is that if we have the faith of the mustard seed we can say to a mountain, "Be thou removed and be cast into the sea", and it will obey us. The humility of Jesus Christ is spoken of here. Remember he is the least of all seeds. We conclude that Christ is the least of all mankind, for the word 'seed' means human being. In other words, if we can empty ourselves out like Christ did, and make ourselves the least like the mustard seed through our obedience to the commandments of God, then we can tell a mountain to move and it will obey us. The mountain could be cancer, AIDS or other sicknesses, or perhaps a marriage breakdown or some other comparable difficulty.

Matthew 13:33 Another parable spake he unto them; The kingdom of heaven is like unto leaven, which a woman took, and hid in three measures of meal, till the whole was leavened.

This parable is also about the kingdom of heaven, yet here it refers to the church. The church is the woman in this parable, likened unto what the apostle Paul wrote in Ephesians 5 concerning the thought of shadows and typologies. The Lord Jesus often spoke on leaven to mean doctrine when he told his disciples to beware of the leaven of the Pharisees, meaning false doctrine. Another understanding Christ gave for leaven was the sin of hypocrisy. Notice that in this parable, the woman hid the leaven in the meal. The meal would be likened to the gospel of Jesus Christ. Through this parable, we understand that the woman (church) is perverting the gospel in these last days, for she is the one putting leaven in the meal. This is why we have so many perverted translations of the bible, and why there are so many cults in the world today.

Matthew 13:44 *Again, the kingdom of heaven is like unto treasure hid in a field; the which when a man hath found, he hideth, and for joy thereof goeth and selleth all that he hath, and buyeth that field.*

The kingdom of heaven is the church in this parable, which is like treasure hid in the field. As the Lord Jesus Christ interpreted the parable of the tares and the wheat, he stated the interpretation of the field meant world (Matthew 13). The man that found the treasure was God, who then paid all that he had to purchase the field. Through the blood of Christ Jesus, a great price was paid to buy the church (treasure in the field) that is the true treasure in this world (1 Corinthians 6:19-20).

Matthew 13:45 Again, the kingdom of heaven is like unto a merchant man, seeking goodly pearls: 46 Who, when he had found one pearl of great price, went and sold all that he had, and bought it.

This parable is about the church (kingdom of heaven). The merchant man is God who is seeking for goodly pearls and found the church (pearl of great price). He then sold all that he had (Jesus Christ), who died to purchase us with his own blood (1 Corinthians 6:19-20).

Matthew 13:52 Then said he unto them, Therefore every scribe which is instructed unto the kingdom of heaven is like unto a man that is an householder, which bringeth forth out of his treasure things new and old.

This parable best explains the preachers and teachers in the church, who are able to teach only out of what they have already studied. This is also a good reason why believers need to read and study the whole word of God. For truly the Holy Ghost will bring to remembrance the doctrines of Christ as we read and study them. This is a great inspiration for teachers and preachers to read the entire word more than once or twice.

Matthew 16:13 *When Jesus came into the coasts of Caesarea Philippi, he asked his disciples, saying, Whom do men say that I the Son of man am? 14 And they said, Some say that thou art John the Baptist: some, Elias; and others, Jeremias, or one of the prophets. 15 He saith unto them, But whom say ye that I am? 16 And Simon Peter answered and said, Thou art the Christ, the Son of the living God. 17 And Jesus answered and said unto him, Blessed art thou, Simon Barjona: for flesh and blood hath not revealed it unto thee, but my Father which is in heaven. 18 And I say also unto thee, That thou art Peter, and upon this rock I will build my church; and the gates* *of hell shall not prevail against it. **19** And I will give unto thee the keys of the kingdom of heaven: and whatsoever thou shalt bind on earth shall be bound in heaven: and whatsoever thou shalt loose on earth shall be loosed in heaven. **20** Then charged he his disciples that they should tell no man that he was Jesus the Christ.*

When Peter answered the question which the Lord Jesus asked, the Lord said he would build the church upon the rock. The apostle John stated that Jesus called Peter "Cephas". The meaning of Cephas is a stone (John 1:42). Therefore when Jesus said upon this Rock I will build my church, he never meant upon Peter. The only Rock in the scriptures is Jesus Christ. He was the Rock that followed the Jews out of Egypt, for forty years (1 Corinthians 10:4). What the Lord Jesus was saying is upon Christ I will build my church. All the scriptures agree that Christ is the corner stone upon which the church is built. He has given unto the Rock the keys of the kingdom of heaven to bind and loose. As believers, we can also have this right through the name of the Lord Jesus Christ to do the same. All disciples of Christ

Jesus who use his name have the key to bind or loose.

Matthew 18:23 *Therefore is the kingdom of heaven likened unto a certain king, which would take account of his servants.* *24 And when he had begun to reckon, one was brought unto him, which owed him ten thousand talents.* *25 But forasmuch as he had not to pay, his lord commanded him to be sold, and his wife, and children, and all that he had, and payment to be made.* *26 The servant therefore fell down, and worshipped him, saying, Lord, have patience with me, and I will pay thee all.* *27 Then the lord of that servant was moved with compassion, and loosed him, and forgave him the debt.* *28 But the same servant went out, and found one of his fellowservants, which owed him an hundred pence: and he laid hands on him, and took him by the throat, saying, Pay me that thou owest.* *29 And his fellowservant fell down at his feet, and besought him, saying, Have patience with me, and I will pay thee all.* *30 And he would not: but went and cast him into prison, till he should pay the debt.* *31 So when his fellowservants saw what was done, they were very sorry, and came and told unto their lord all that was done. 32 Then his lord, after that he had called him, said unto him, O thou wicked servant, I forgave thee all that debt, because thou desiredst me: 33 Shouldest not thou also have had compassion on thy fellowservant, even as I had pity on thee? 34 And his lord was wroth, and delivered him to the tormentors, till he should pay all that was due unto him. 35 So likewise shall my heavenly Father do also unto you, if ye from your hearts forgive not every one his brother their trespasses.*

In this manifestation of the kingdom of heaven, all believers in the church receive one or more talents. Although we cannot physically see those talents which are within us, the manifestation is open to all. This parable is also about the church of Jesus Christ, which is the kingdom of heaven. In the church, Christ Jesus is the king who forgave all those who were indebted to him. Every sinner therefore is indebted to God, and their sin is so deep in trespasses that none can pay the debt. God had to forgive everyone his sin through the blood of Jesus Christ. Once a person is forgiven of all his sin, God expects that person to do what was done unto them. They are commanded to forgive everyone else that is indebted to them, whatever the debt is. If they have been raped, molested, cheated on, abused, stolen from, or lied about, all debt is to be forgiven. The story tells every sinner that God forgave their own sin and now they need to forgive every one who is indebted to them. Now consider how much sin was forgiven from our birth. So no matter what another person has done to sin against us, it still is not as much sin as God forgave us of.

The parable informs us that if we do not forgive, God will then turn us over to the tormentors. In some instances, the tormentors could be those who will physically torment us, like Israel was turned over to their enemies for their unrepented sins. This is why Israel had many people oppress them or bring them into bondage.

On the other hand, sometimes God would send in a different kind of tormentor, instead of the human kind. One story tells us that because Israel sinned, God sent in fiery serpents that bit the children of Israel. The metaphoric thought leads us to understand that the Lord sent in the devils to torment them to bring about repentance (1 Corinthians 5:1-5). Although we may not see the tormentors (devils, sicknesses, etc.), this explains why many Christians suffer today without physical healing. Furthermore, although people may anoint them or pray for them to be healed, nothing happens sometimes due to unforgiveness. Nevertheless, once they repent of the unforgiveness it would appear that God will then deliver them again.

Here is another revelation of the church of Jesus Christ, for this first manifestation.

Matthew 20:1 For the kingdom of heaven is like unto a man that is an householder, which went out early in the morning to hire labourers into his vineyard. 2 And when he had agreed with the labourers for a penny a day, he sent them into his vineyard. 3 And he went out about the third hour, and saw others standing idle in the marketplace, 4 And said unto them; Go ye also into the vineyard, and whatsoever is right I will give you. And they went their way. 5 Again he went out about the sixth and ninth hour, and did likewise. 6 And about the eleventh hour he went out, and found others standing idle, and saith unto them, Why stand ye here all the day idle? 7 They say unto him, Because no man hath hired us. He saith unto them, Go ye also into the vineyard; and whatsoever is right, that shall ye receive. 8 So when even was come, the lord of the vineyard saith unto his steward, Call the labourers, and give them their hire, beginning from the last unto the first. 9 And when they came that were hired about the eleventh hour, they received every man a penny. 10 But when the first came, they supposed that they should have received more; and they likewise received every man a penny. 11 And when they had received it, they murmured against the goodman of the house, 12 Saying, These last have wrought but one hour, and thou hast made them equal unto us, which have borne the burden and heat of the day. 13 But he answered one of them, and said, Friend, I do thee no wrong: didst not thou agree with me for a penny? 14 Take that thine is, and go thy way: I will give unto this last, even as unto thee. 15 Is it not lawful for me to do what I will with mine own? Is thine eye evil, because I am good? 16 So the last shall be first, and the first last: for many be called, but few chosen.

Every one in the kingdom of heaven today is called to work in the vineyard. The manifestation of our work is spiritual, and so is the reward that we will receive at the judgment seat of Christ (2 Corinthians 5:10). Whether we work for fifty years or only two years, we are all going to receive the same reward of salvation, and the wage given to the laborers in the parable represents this salvation.

When we come before the judgment seat of Christ at the end of the great tribulation, many disciples will receive more talents, more authority, more crowns, and a greater resurrection than others. This is a true statement about rewards; some Christians will receive more than others. The reason is that their labor was greater, while others did not labor as much. This does not contradict the parable about the kingdom of heaven because the one wage that all believers receive alike is salvation.

Whenever we look at resemblances of the church of Jesus Christ as the kingdom of heaven, we learn much more about the faith. Another parable will help us to learn about the manifestation of the kingdom of heaven.

Matthew 21:28 But what think ye? A certain man had two sons; and he came to the first, and said, Son, go work to day in my vineyard. 29 He answered and said, I will not: but afterward he repented, and went. 30 And he came to the second, and said likewise. And he answered and said, I go, sir: and went not. 31 Whether of them twain did the will of his father? They say unto him, The first. Jesus saith unto them, Verily I say unto you, That the publicans and the harlots go into the kingdom of God before you. 32 For John came unto you in the way of righteousness, and ye believed him not: but the publicans and the harlots believed him: and ye, when ye had seen it, repented not afterward, that ye might believe him.

The interpretation of the word of God concerning the last being first and the first being last is made even clearer by this parable. Whenever religious people make themselves first they will become last. Although the Jewish leaders heard John preach about the gospel, they would not repent, yet whenever the sinners heard him they repented. Many of the Jewish leaders lost their opportunity to receive the kingdom. Although these leaders studied the scriptures thinking of themselves as first, they became last. The scripture was fulfilled, whereby even the harlots came before these religious leaders.

Each parable of the kingdom of heaven gives us greater insight about the church, or Christ, or God.

Matthew 21:33 *Hear another parable: There was a certain householder, which planted a vineyard, and hedged it round about, and digged a winepress in it, and built a tower, and let it out to husbandmen, and went into a far country: **34** And when the time of the fruit drew near, he sent his servants to the husbandmen, that they might receive the fruits of it. **35** And the husbandmen took his servants, and beat one, and killed another, and stoned another. **36** Again, he sent other servants more than the first: and they did unto them likewise. **37** But last of all he sent unto* *them his son, saying, They will reverence my son. 38 But when the husbandmen saw the son, they said among themselves, This is the heir; come, let us kill him, and let us seize on his inheritance. 39 And they caught him, and cast him out of the vineyard, and slew him. 40 When the lord therefore of the vineyard cometh, what will he do unto those husbandmen? 41 They say unto him, He will miserably destroy those wicked men, and will let out his vineyard unto other husbandmen, which shall render him the fruits in their seasons. 42 Jesus saith unto them, Did ye never read in the scriptures, The stone which the builders rejected, the same is become the head of the corner: this is the Lord's doing, and it is marvellous in our eyes? 43 Therefore say I unto you, The kingdom of God shall be taken from you, and given to a nation bringing forth the fruits thereof. 44 And whosoever shall fall on this stone shall be broken: but on whomsoever it shall fall, it will grind him to powder.*

In this parable about the kingdom of heaven (church) we learn two things. The parable leads us to understand how the Jewish people lost the kingdom and the Gentiles received it.

During this manifestation of the kingdom of heaven, we can clearly discern how we have been given the kingdom of heaven as the church of Jesus Christ. The Jews should have given to the Lord the fruits of the kingdom. However, instead of bearing fruit they killed the servants of God. The Lord Jesus taught in the metaphor that he was a vine and we are his branches. As branches, we are commanded to bring forth fruit.

Now if Christ is the vine, he is also understood to be the word of God. If the life flows through the vine into the branches, then the only way for a Christian to bear fruit is to become a doer of the word of God. Each time we obey the doctrine of Christ we are bearing fruit. Just as the apostle Paul taught, whenever we support the ministry it is obedience to the gospel and therefore is fruit-bearing (Philippians 4:15-17). Moreover, if we look into the language of shadows and typologies, bearing fruit would be likened to the nature of God. Whenever we are in the Holy Ghost and bring forth love, joy, peace, gentleness, goodness, temperance, faith, etc. we are bearing fruit (Galatians 5:22-23).

Even the Lord Jesus Christ was murdered

by the Jews, because they thought they could keep the kingdom for themselves. Nevertheless, the kingdom belongs to the Son. God therefore took the kingdom from the Jewish people and gave it to all believers, both Jews and Gentiles, who will bring forth the fruits of the vineyard.

In the end times, God will pour out his wrath upon the Jews and this parable gives us the same insight. God will destroy the Jewish people, sending the anti-Christ (2 Thessalonians 2:8-12) who will tread down Israel (great tribulation) for forty two months (Revelation 11:2). Those in the kingdom have fallen upon the stone (Jesus Christ) through believing Christ Jesus died for their sins. Yet the manifestation of the stone spoken of here will fall upon those who reject salvation through the death of Christ. Perhaps we will not see it with these eyes, but nevertheless the stone will grind them to powder. One day all Israel will be saved and turn to the one they rejected, but not before they receive the anti-Christ as messiah and go through the great tribulation.

Matthew 22:1 And Jesus answered and spake

unto them again by parables, and said, 2 The kingdom of heaven is like unto a certain king, which made a marriage for his son, 3 And sent forth his servants to call them that were bidden to the wedding: and they would not come. 4 Again, he sent forth other servants, saying, Tell them which are bidden, Behold, I have prepared my dinner: my oxen and my fatlings are killed, and all things are ready: come unto the marriage. 5 But they made light of it, and went their ways, one to his farm, another to his merchandise: 6 And the remnant took his servants, and entreated them spitefully, and slew them. 7 But when the king heard thereof, he was wroth: and he sent forth his armies, and destroyed those murderers, and burned up their city. 8 Then saith he to his servants, The wedding is ready, but they which were bidden were not worthy. 9 Go ye therefore into the highways, and as many as ye shall find, bid to the marriage. 10 So those servants went out into the highways, and gathered together all as many as they found, both bad and good: and the wedding was furnished with guests. 11 And when the king came in to see the guests, he saw there a man which had not on a

Kingdom Theology

*wedding garment: **12** And he saith unto him, Friend, how camest thou in hither not having a wedding garment? And he was speechless. **13** Then said the king to the servants, Bind him hand and foot, and take him away, and cast him into outer darkness; there shall be weeping and gnashing of teeth. **14** For many are called, but few are chosen.*

In this parable about the kingdom of heaven, the marriage of Christ Jesus and the bride is God's will. The manifestation of this parable has already happened to Israel as the prophets of old and apostles preached to the Jewish people. Though the servants went to the Jewish people first, they rejected the message and refused to repent by preparing for the marriage. The Lord made comment about the Jewish people killing his messengers that were sent unto them. Therefore the Lord sends out his armies and destroys those murderous people. Afterwards the servants of the Lord (apostles and disciples) are sent to all people to prepare for the wedding of Christ.

The manifestation that appears today is the thousands of witnesses world-wide testifying to the grace of God and salvation through

Christ alone. Those who come to the wedding are Christians, both Jews and Gentiles. The wedding has not yet taken place. For the past two thousand years, all the guests have been waiting for the wedding of the Son in heaven.

The preparation for the wedding is a godly lifestyle that allows the Christian to put on a wedding garment.

Revelation 19:7 *Let us be glad and rejoice, and give honour to him: for the marriage of the Lamb is come, and his wife hath made herself ready.* ***8*** *And to her was granted that she should be arrayed in fine linen, clean and white: for the fine linen is the righteousness of saints.*

On the wedding dayof Christ, those who enter without a wedding garment are dragged out and bound hand and foot. It would appear that the wedding garment is only obtained while the believer is on earth. Righteousness or obedience to the gospel is what will be rewarded with a wedding garment. Today we cannot physically see this wedding garment on believers, but the manifestation is apparent in their new nature. Somehow, there will be those who make it into the feast without the wedding garment. They will later be dragged out in the presence of the Father, Son, and saints.

We realize that in the church (kingdom of heaven), since its origin, are those who live godly lives and those who do not obey the gospel. Yet the gospel of the kingdom of heaven has been preached since the time Christ Jesus arose from the dead. In the last days (tribulation period), the gospel of the kingdom of heaven will be preached as the main message of the saints.

Matthew 24:14 And this gospel of the kingdom shall be preached in all the world for a witness unto all nations; and then shall the end come.

The gospel of the kingdom shall be preached before the end of the tribulation period. This prophesy tells us as believers that the last message to be preached by the saints before Jesus returns will be mostly about the kingdom of heaven.

I believe we are seeing and understanding more about the kingdom of heaven today than in days gone by. The reason according to our text is that Christ Jesus will soon return with the next kingdom of heaven and we must prepare. Furthermore, this scripture teaches us that if the kingdom of heaven is being preached during the great tribulation, then the body of Jesus Christ is still in the earth.

The reason I make this statement is simple: the gospel will not be preached by the unsaved but rather by the saved. Although I believe in a rapture of the faithful saints, not all believers will be caught up. Again, once someone receives salvation during the great tribulation, they become part of the body of Christ.

We conclude then that the first rapture is for the bride only, rather than for the body of Jesus Christ. This is a bold statement and can be easily backed up by the word of God, as this verse and many others teach about the gospel being preached during the great tribulation.

Here is another parable on the same matter of the rapture taking away the bride, but leaving the body behind.

Matthew 25:1 *Then shall the kingdom of heaven be likened unto ten virgins, which took* *their lamps, and went forth to meet the bridegroom. 2 And five of them were wise, and five were foolish. 3 They that were foolish took their lamps, and took no oil with them: 4 But the wise took oil in their vessels with their lamps. 5 While the bridegroom tarried, they all slumbered and slept. 6 And at midnight there was a cry made, Behold, the bridegroom cometh; go ye out to meet him. 7 Then all those virgins arose, and trimmed their lamps. 8 And the foolish said unto the wise, Give us of your oil; for our lamps are gone out. 9 But the wise answered, saying, Not so; lest there be not enough for us and you: but go ye rather to them that sell, and buy for yourselves. 10 And while they went to buy, the bridegroom came; and they that were ready went in with him to the marriage: and the door was shut. 11 Afterward came also the other virgins, saying, Lord, Lord, open to us. 12 But he answered and said, Verily I say unto you, I know you not. 13 Watch therefore, for ye know neither the day nor the hour wherein the Son of man cometh.*

The Lord Jesus Christ is likening his church to the kingdom of heaven, saying that the church contains ten virgins.   This metaphor instructs us that all believers have no more sin, but are considered virgins by God. The Lord makes a distinction however between the body of Christ and the bride of Christ. While the body of Christ is all ten virgins, the bride of Christ is only five wise virgins.

Each virgin has a lamp, which is the word of God as King David said in Psalms 119:105, "thy word is a lamp unto my feet". This is also another metaphoric name of Jesus Christ (John 1:1). Every saint has Christ (the Word) inside of them.

In this parable about the church, not all saints have oil in their lamps, which refers to the Holy Ghost. Although every believer has the Holy Ghost upon salvation (Ephesians 1:13), not all believers have an anointing. This oil represents the anointing in the believer's life, which a saint can increase through bible study, prayer, drawing near to God, living a godly life, obeying the gospel and praying in tongues. The foolish virgins trying to buy oil are in the church today, and some of those with the anointing oil are willing to sell it to the foolish virgins.

This explains why we pay to hear the gospel being taught in some seminars by anointed preachers, instead of 'freely ye received freely give'. Furthermore, some anointed singers sell their oil to the foolish virgins just as readily as preachers do. The foolish virgins are those saints who will not fast, live godly lives, obey the gospel, and so on. They therefore try to buy the anointing oil. These wise and foolish virgins may be found in all churches and denominations today, not to mention the sellers of oil.

When the bridegroom returns (Jesus Christ), he does not take all the body of Christ with him (rapture), but only those saints who were ready for the wedding. Notice the cry was made, "Go out to meet him." I believe this is a reference to those saints who go out of this world's beliefs, leaving behind the sin of the world with all its lust, in order to prepare to meet Christ. The foolish virgins and the sellers of oil are left behind, as the bride is raptured at the midnight hour. The midnight hour is explained as some period during the seven year tribulation, when darkness has already covered the earth. This is not the second coming of Christ, but is more commonly known as the secret coming of Christ.

Matthew 25:14 *For the kingdom of heaven is as a man travelling into a far country, who called his own servants, and delivered unto them his goods.* **15** *And unto one he gave five talents, to another two, and to another one; to every man according to his several ability; and straightway took his journey.* **16** *Then he that had received the five talents went and traded with the same, and made them other five talents.* **17** *And likewise he that had received two, he also gained other two.* **18** *But he that had received one went and digged in the earth, and hid his lord's money.* **19** *After a long time the lord of those servants cometh, and reckoneth with them.* **20** *And so he that had received five talents came and brought other five talents, saying, Lord, thou deliveredst unto me five talents: behold, I have gained beside them five talents more.* **21** *His lord said unto him, Well done, thou good and faithful servant: thou hast been faithful over a few things, I will make thee ruler over many things: enter thou into the joy of thy lord.* **22** *He also that had received two talents came and said, Lord, thou deliveredst unto me two talents: behold, I have gained two* *other talents beside them. 23 His lord said unto him, Well done, good and faithful servant; thou hast been faithful over a few things, I will make thee ruler over many things: enter thou into the joy of thy lord. 24 Then he which had received the one talent came and said, Lord, I knew thee that thou art an hard man, reaping where thou hast not sown, and gathering where thou hast not strawed: 25 And I was afraid, and went and hid thy talent in the earth: lo, there thou hast that is thine. 26 His lord answered and said unto him, Thou wicked and slothful servant, thou knewest that I reap where I sowed not, and gather where I have not strawed: 27 Thou oughtest therefore to have put my money to the exchangers, and then at my coming I should have received mine own with usury. 28 Take therefore the talent from him, and give it unto him which hath ten talents. 29 For unto every one that hath shall be given, and he shall have abundance: but from him that hath not shall be taken away even that which he hath. 30 And cast ye the unprofitable servant into outer darkness: there shall be weeping and gnashing of teeth.*

Luke 19:11 *And as they heard these things,*

he added and spake a parable, because he was nigh to Jerusalem, and because they thought that the kingdom of God should immediately appear. 12 He said therefore, A certain nobleman went into a far country to receive for himself a kingdom, and to return. 13 And he called his ten servants, and delivered them ten pounds, and said unto them, Occupy till I come. 14 But his citizens hated him, and sent a message after him, saying, We will not have this man to reign over us. 15 And it came to pass, that when he was returned, having received the kingdom, then he commanded these servants to be called unto him, to whom he had given the money, that he might know how much every man had gained by trading. 16 Then came the first, saying, Lord, thy pound hath gained ten pounds. 17 And he said unto him, Well, thou good servant: because thou hast been faithful in a very little, have thou authority over ten cities. 18 And the second came, saying, Lord, thy pound hath gained five pounds. 19 And he said likewise to him, Be thou also over five cities. 20 And another came, saying, Lord, behold, here is thy pound, which I have kept laid up in a napkin: 21 For

Kingdom Theology

I feared thee, because thou art an austere man: thou takest up that thou layedst not down, and reapest that thou didst not sow. 22 And he saith unto him, Out of thine own mouth will I judge thee, thou wicked servant. Thou knewest that I was an austere man, taking up that I laid not down, and reaping that I did not sow: 23 Wherefore then gavest not thou my money into the bank, that at my coming I might have required mine own with usury? 24 And he said unto them that stood by, Take from him the pound, and give it to him that hath ten pounds. 25 (And they said unto him, Lord, he hath ten pounds.) 26 For I say unto you, That unto every one which hath shall be given; and from him that hath not, even that he hath shall be taken away from him. 27 But those mine enemies, which would not that I should reign over them, bring hither, and slay them before me.

The Lord Jesus testifies to every believer in the kingdom that they have received a talent from God. The one talent that all believers have received is salvation; therefore, they can become witnesses for Christ. However, there are those in the church who receive more than one talent and must use them for the saving of souls, or edifying the church. We must realize that this parable also teaches that the saints will have their talents until Christ returns with the next kingdom of heaven. They cannot lose their talents, as some think possible today, for the gifts and calling of God are without repentance.

Nevertheless, they could bury their talents by living carnally, as the apostle explains in 1 Corinthians 3. The Lord Jesus also made a similar statement when he said not to put our light under a bushel. This means we must not live in the flesh, but in the spirit, for if we live in the flesh we bury our talent or hide our light.

At the second coming of Christ Jesus, those who gained other talents all heard the same blessing as a reward, " Enter into the joy of the Lord." I believe that this statement refers to those saints who will rule on the earth during the millennium. This is the joy of the Lord which Jesus spoke of. The man that buried his talent will be dragged out in the presence of the Lamb. This man represents numerous people like the woman represents the church. Some manifest their talents openly in the church today, while others ignore all warnings and bury their talent.

Matthew 25:31 When the Son of man shall come in his glory, and all the holy angels with him, then shall he sit upon the throne of his glory: 32 And before him shall be gathered all nations: and he shall separate them one from another, as a shepherd divideth his sheep from the goats: 33 And he shall set the sheep on his right hand, but the goats on the left. 34 Then shall the King say unto them on his right hand, Come, ye blessed of my Father, inherit the kingdom prepared for you from the foundation of the world: 35 For I was an hungred, and ye gave me meat: I was thirsty, and ye gave me drink: I was a stranger, and ye took me in: 36 Naked, and ye clothed me: I was sick, and ye visited me: I was in prison, and ye came unto me. 37 Then shall the righteous answer him, saying, Lord, when saw we thee an hungred, and fed thee? or thirsty, and gave thee drink? 38 When saw we thee a stranger, and took thee in? or naked, and clothed thee? 39 Or when saw we thee sick, or in prison, and came unto thee? 40 And the King shall answer and say unto them, Verily I say unto you, Inasmuch as ye have done it unto one of the least of these my brethren, ye have done it unto me. 41 Then shall he say also unto them on the left hand, Depart from me, ye cursed, into everlasting fire, prepared for the devil and his angels: 42 For I was an hungred, and ye gave me no meat: I was thirsty, and ye gave me no drink: 43 I was a stranger, and ye took me not in: naked, and ye clothed me not: sick, and in prison, and ye visited me not. 44 Then shall they also answer him, saying, Lord, when saw we thee an hungred, or athirst, or a stranger, or naked, or sick, or in prison, and did not minister unto thee? 45 Then shall he answer them, saying, Verily I say unto you, Inasmuch as ye did it not to one of the least of these, ye did it not to me. 46 And these shall go away into everlasting punishment: but the righteous into life eternal.

At the second coming of Christ, he will judge his church and reward all those who laboured during their earthly lives. This story about the kingdom of heaven explains those who are living as sheep in the kingdom today, and those least saints who are in need of ministry. Today, some believers are feeding those least saints, or visiting them in prisons and hospitals. This is the manifestation of the kingdom of heaven in the believer's life. Their righteousness shall be rewarded at the second coming of Christ, as they will be able to inherit the millennial kingdom of heaven. The Christians who were in need of being visited in the hospital, or in the prison, or found to be naked, were not told that they would go to hell or that they would inherit the millennial kingdom. The goats are explained as those religious people in the church who do not care for the saints, and I personally believe they have not been born again. It would appear these goats have but an appearance of godliness, without the power.

Notes:_____

_____

_____

_____

_____

_____

_____

_____

_____

_____

First Dispensation of the Kingdom of God

The first dispensation of the kingdom of God started when Jesus Christ died on the cross, and will last until he returns with the next kingdom of heaven. We could safely state that the first dispensation is for two thousand years, ending at the second coming of Christ Jesus. Let us therefore turn back to some of the scriptures we have previously studied for understanding of the manifestation of the kingdom of God, and learn from them concerning this dispensation.

Mark 9:1 *And he said unto them, Verily I say unto you, That there be some of them that stand here, which shall not taste of death, till they have seen the kingdom of God come with power.*

We must understand the clarity of this verse and what the Lord was saying in this passage of scripture. First, he was talking to those

disciples who lived two thousand years ago.
Secondly, he told them that they would not
die until the kingdom came with power. In
order for this prophesy of Christ Jesus to be
true, only two explanations could be
understood from this verse. Either the
kingdom of God did come while they were
still alive two thousand years ago, or else the
kingdom spoken of here refers to the
millennial kingdom, and those disciples are
still alive somewhere waiting for the kingdom
to come. Personally, I do not believe that
those disciples are alive today. So the
kingdom of God referred to here must have
come already while those men were alive.

Here is another teaching of the Lord Jesus
Christ concerning the dispensation of the first
kingdom.

*John 3:3 Jesus answered and said unto him,
Verily, verily, I say unto thee, Except a man
be born again, he cannot see the kingdom of
God. 4 Nicodemus saith unto him, How can a
man be born when he is old? can he enter the
second time into his mother's womb, and be
born? 5 Jesus answered, Verily, verily, I say
unto thee, Except a man be born of water and*

of the Spirit, he cannot enter into the kingdom of God.

This religious leader could not discern the meaning of the words of the Lord Jesus. That is why he asked a foolish question. However, the Lord Jesus points out that the kingdom of heaven came when he died on the cross. This is why he states a man cannot see the kingdom in verse 3, or enter the kingdom of heaven unless he is born again.

Another term we need to consider is the word "see", which is used to mean our understanding or perception. Once we are born again, we start to comprehend the laws of sowing and reaping in the kingdom of God, not to mention our authority, and the power of the kingdom.

Once a person is born again, he enters the kingdom of heaven. This entrance into the kingdom was made possible after Jesus Christ died on the cross. We conclude that salvation and entering the kingdom of God were granted to those disciples who did not die, but entered that kingdom of God during their lifetimes. Furthermore, the apostle Paul confirms that the kingdom of heaven is here already, and we have entered into it.

Kingdom Theology

Nicodemus asked the right question to Jesus, on how to become born again. The reason is that being born again is the requirement for entrance into this first kingdom of heaven. Notice the Lord taught that you cannot understand (see) the kingdom of heaven if you are not born again Unless someone is born again, he could never understand the laws of the kingdom, like sowing and reaping, blessing and cursing, power and authority (John 3:3).

No one can enter the kingdom of heaven unless they are born again; once they become born again, they enter the kingdom of heaven immediately (John 3:5).

The kingdom of heaven is also called the kingdom of God, or the kingdom of Christ. It is the same kingdom which the Lord refers to, only given different names. Once a person enters the kingdom of God, he is translated out of the devil's kingdom, into Christ's kingdom. Receiving God's kingdom, we should serve as those in the kingdom. The scriptures teach that we are citizens of Christ's kingdom, given all the authority to use the name of the king in the kingdom (Hebrews 12:28 & Ephesians 2:19).

Kingdom Theology

Colossians 1:12 *Giving thanks unto the Father, which hath made us meet to be partakers of the inheritance of the saints in light: **13** Who hath delivered us from the power of darkness, and hath translated us into the kingdom of his dear Son:*

When we received Christ as our savior, we were translated into the kingdom. God translated us out of the devil's kingdom, into the kingdom of his dear Son.

This is also seen in a parallel truth, as Israel left the Pharaoh's kingdom. In order for the Jews to leave Egypt, they needed the blood of the lamb. In order for people to leave the devil's kingdom, they need the blood of the lamb. The very day the blood is applied we walk out of Pharaoh's kingdom, or as believers we should understand we leave Satan's kingdom. We are already in the kingdom of heaven now, as a result of being born again. Although our physical body is still mortal, our spirit has been translated into the kingdom of God.

The parables also explain in more detail the dispensation of the kingdom of God.

Kingdom Theology

Luke 19:11 And as they heard these things, he added and spake a parable, because he was nigh to Jerusalem, and because they thought that the kingdom of God should immediately appear. 12 He said therefore, A certain nobleman went into a far country to receive for himself a kingdom, and to return. 13 And he called his ten servants, and delivered them ten pounds, and said unto them, Occupy till I come. 14 But his citizens hated him, and sent a message after him, saying, We will not have this man to reign over us. 15 And it came to pass, that when he was returned, having received the kingdom, then he commanded these servants to be called unto him, to whom he had given the money, that he might know how much every man had gained by trading. 16 Then came the first, saying, Lord, thy pound hath gained ten pounds. 17 And he said unto him, Well, thou good servant: because thou hast been faithful in a very little, have thou authority over ten cities. 18 And the second came, saying, Lord, thy pound hath gained five pounds. 19 And he said likewise to him, Be thou also over five cities. 20 And another came, saying, Lord, behold, here is thy pound, which I have kept laid up in a napkin: 21 For I feared thee, because thou art an austere man: thou takest up that thou layedst not down, and reapest that thou didst not sow. 22 And he saith unto him, Out of thine own mouth will I judge thee, thou wicked servant. Thou knewest that I was an austere man, taking up that I laid not down, and reaping that I did not sow: 23 Wherefore then gavest not thou my money into the bank, that at my coming I might have required mine own with usury? 24 And he said unto them that stood by, Take from him the pound, and give it to him that hath ten pounds. 25 (And they said unto him, Lord, he hath ten pounds.) 26 For I say unto you, That unto every one which hath shall be given; and from him that hath not, even that he hath shall be taken away from him. 27 But those mine enemies, which would not that I should reign over them, bring hither, and slay them before me.

The Lord Jesus starts to explain this parable based on the thought that those who were there that day believed the kingdom of God should immediately appear. Although in other parables Christ taught that the kingdom would soon come, he now deals with the beginning of the millennial kingdom in this parable. The very beginning of this parable explains the ending of the first dispensation, and the beginning of the second dispensation. The Lord Jesus Christ leaves the earth and goes into a far country (heaven) to receive a kingdom which is known as the millennial kingdom of heaven.

Notes:_____

_____

_____

_____

_____

_____

_____

_____

_____

_____

_____

_____

_____

_____

_____

_____

_____

Kingdom Theology

Second Manifestation of the Kingdom

The second manifestation of the kingdom of heaven is a physical kingdom that will control all the kingdoms of the earth. The government of all kingdoms will rest upon the shoulders of Jesus Christ, and he will rule all nations from Jerusalem for one thousand years. All those saints who died in Christ will be given glorified bodies, in order to serve as kings and priests for one thousand years with Jesus Christ. During this millennium, people will still be marrying and given in marriage. Death will also be present until this last enemy is destroyed at the end of the millennium. The animals' nature will return to how they were created as vegetarians. Devils will be cast into hell along with Satan during the millennium. People will live longer until the scripture is fulfilled which says a child shall die at one hundred years old.

As this kingdom is ending, Satan is set free from hell and deceives Gog and Magog into attacking the saints in Israel. Fire comes down from God out of heaven, ending that war and the dispensation.

Let us consider some scriptures concerning this manifestation.

***Isaiah 9:6** For unto us a child is born, unto us a son is given: and the government shall be upon his shoulder: and his name shall be called Wonderful, Counsellor, The mighty God, The everlasting Father, The Prince of Peace. 7 Of the increase of his government and peace there shall be no end, upon the throne of David, and upon his kingdom, to order it, and to establish it with judgment and with justice from henceforth even for ever. The zeal of the LORD of hosts will perform this.*

From these verses we readily understand that the millennial kingdom is a physical one, which the Lord Jesus Christ will rule as the son of David. Notice that the prophet stated the government shall rest upon his shoulders, testifying to a physical kingdom which will rule the whole earth. The prophesy from Nathan concerning David's son ruling the kingdom of Israel is still coming to pass during this next kingdom of heaven (2 Samuel 7:12-13). The prophesy starts at the first dispensation of the kingdom of heaven and continues during this next dispensation. The outward appearance of the kingdom is open for all to witness, as the kingdoms of the world will become the kingdoms of Christ. This manifestation is a government to rule the whole earth.

Luke 21:31 So likewise ye, when ye see these things come to pass, know ye that the kingdom of God is nigh at hand.

The prophesy of the Lord Jesus Christ concerning the second manifestation of the kingdom of God was that the millennial kingdom of God is near when certain signs come to pass. The three major categories of signs which Christ spoke of here are 1) the beginning of sorrows, 2) the three and one-half year tribulation and 3) the three and one-half year great tribulation.

As the great tribulation ends, the millennial

kingdom of heaven begins.

Revelation 11:15 *And the seventh angel sounded; and there were great voices in heaven, saying, The kingdoms of this world are become the kingdoms of our Lord, and of his Christ; and he shall reign for ever and ever.*

From this verse we can state with assurance that once Christ Jesus returns, a theocracy will dominate the world, not democracy. Although all the kingdoms of the world become the kingdoms of Christ, there is no mention of changing the languages of any nation. Rather Isaiah informs us that languages will continue during the millennial kingdom of Christ.

Luke 1:26 *And in the sixth month the angel Gabriel was sent from God unto a city of Galilee, named Nazareth, 27 To a virgin espoused to a man whose name was Joseph, of the house of David; and the virgin's name was Mary. 28 And the angel came in unto her, and said, Hail, thou that art highly favoured, the Lord is with thee: blessed art thou among women. 29 And when she saw him, she was troubled at his saying, and cast in her mind* *what manner of salutation this should be.* ***30*** *And the angel said unto her, Fear not, Mary: for thou hast found favour with God.* ***31*** *And, behold, thou shalt conceive in thy womb, and bring forth a son, and shalt call his name JESUS.* ***32*** *He shall be great, and shall be called the Son of the Highest: and the Lord God shall give unto him the throne of his father David:* ***33*** *And he shall reign over the house of Jacob for ever; and of his kingdom there shall be no end.*

This prophesy, spoken to Mary concerning the Lord Jesus Christ, informs us that God's plan from the days beyond king David was to have Jesus Christ rule the world from Jerusalem. His kingdom started at Calvary within the heart of man, as we have already seen, but this second manifestation is an outward manifestation seen by the entire world.

Isaiah 11:1 *And there shall come forth a rod out of the stem of Jesse, and a Branch shall grow out of his roots:* ***2*** *And the spirit of the LORD shall rest upon him, the spirit of wisdom and understanding, the spirit of counsel and might, the spirit of knowledge* *and of the fear of the LORD; 3 And shall make him of quick understanding in the fear of the LORD: and he shall not judge after the sight of his eyes, neither reprove after the hearing of his ears: 4 But with righteousness shall he judge the poor, and reprove with equity for the meek of the earth: and he shall smite the earth with the rod of his mouth, and with the breath of his lips shall he slay the wicked. 5 And righteousness shall be the girdle of his loins, and faithfulness the girdle of his reins. 6 The wolf also shall dwell with the lamb, and the leopard shall lie down with the kid; and the calf and the young lion and the fatling together; and a little child shall lead them. 7 And the cow and the bear shall feed; their young ones shall lie down together: and the lion shall eat straw like the ox. 8 And the sucking child shall play on the hole of the asp, and the weaned child shall put his hand on the cockatrice' den. 9 They shall not hurt nor destroy in all my holy mountain: for the earth shall be full of the knowledge of the LORD, as the waters cover the sea. 10 And in that day there shall be a root of Jesse, which shall stand for an ensign of the people; to it shall the Gentiles seek:*

and his rest shall be glorious. 11 And it shall come to pass in that day, that the Lord shall set his hand again the second time to recover the remnant of his people, which shall be left, from Assyria, and from Egypt, and from Pathros, and from Cush, and from Elam, and from Shinar, and from Hamath, and from the islands of the sea. 12 And he shall set up an ensign for the nations, and shall assemble the outcasts of Israel, and gather together the dispersed of Judah from the four corners of the earth.

In the first few verses, Isaiah informs us of Christ as the son of David, who will rule the nations. For truly he is the rod from the stem of Jesse, king David's father. Once his millennial kingdom begins, the animals' nature will become vegetarian again, as when they were created. Notice the lion will eat straw like the ox, and the wolf and the lamb shall dwell together. During the millennium, the earth will be filled with the knowledge of God. Also notice the root of Jesse (being Jesus Christ) will be sought by the Gentiles, who will be granted a glorious rest as they follow his gospel. All Israel will be saved and come to the knowledge of God, that Jesus

Christ is the Messiah.

Isaiah 14:7 The whole earth is at rest, and is quiet: they break forth into singing. 8 Yea, the fir trees rejoice at thee, and the cedars of Lebanon, saying, Since thou art laid down, no feller is come up against us. 9 Hell from beneath is moved for thee to meet thee at thy coming: it stirreth up the dead for thee, even all the chief ones of the earth; it hath raised up from their thrones all the kings of the nations. 10 All they shall speak and say unto thee, Art thou also become weak as we? art thou become like unto us? 11 Thy pomp is brought down to the grave, and the noise of thy viols: the worm is spread under thee, and the worms cover thee. 12 How art thou fallen from heaven, O Lucifer, son of the morning! how art thou cut down to the ground, which didst weaken the nations! 13 For thou hast said in thine heart, I will ascend into heaven, I will exalt my throne above the stars of God: I will sit also upon the mount of the congregation, in the sides of the north: 14 I will ascend above the heights of the clouds; I will be like the most High. 15 Yet thou shalt be brought down to hell, to the sides of the pit. 16 They that see thee shall narrowly look upon thee, and consider thee, saying, Is this the man that made the earth to tremble, that did shake kingdoms; 17 That made the world as a wilderness, and destroyed the cities thereof; that opened not the house of his prisoners? 18 All the kings of the nations, even all of them, lie in glory, every one in his own house. 19 But thou art cast out of thy grave like an abominable branch, and as the raiment of those that are slain, thrust through with a sword, that go down to the stones of the pit; as a carcase trodden under feet. 20 Thou shalt not be joined with them in burial, because thou hast destroyed thy land, and slain thy people: the seed of evildoers shall never be renowned.

Notice in verse 7 the earth is finally at rest. The reason is revealed in the later verses; Satan is no longer on the earth. Perhaps the closest understanding we could have of the millennial reign of Christ would be a comparison to King Solomon, who had rest from all his enemies during his reign. In verse 9 and down, we understand that when Jesus Christ returns, Satan will be bound in hell for one thousand years. The description of what happens to the devil during the millennium is opened up to us here in these verses. The kings already in hell are wondering what happened to the devil, asking if he has become as weak as they are. The period for Lucifer to be thrown down to hell is found in the book of Revelation.

***Revelation 20:1** And I saw an angel come down from heaven, having the key of the bottomless pit and a great chain in his hand. **2** And he laid hold on the dragon, that old serpent, which is the Devil, and Satan, and bound him a thousand years, **3** And cast him into the bottomless pit, and shut him up, and set a seal upon him, that he should deceive the nations no more, till the thousand years should be fulfilled: and after that he must be loosed a little season.*

The apostle John informs us that Satan would be bound during the millennium with a great chain and thrown into the bottomless pit. The bottomless pit is another name for hell, or Sheol, or the pit.

Just as Satan will be bound at the second coming of Christ by the angel of the Lord, another event will also take place known as the first resurrection. This happens just before the millennium begins.

John 5:28 Marvel not at this: for the hour is coming, in the which all that are in the graves shall hear his voice, 29 And shall come forth; they that have done good, unto the resurrection of life; and they that have done evil, unto the resurrection of damnation.

The first mention of the resurrection was from the Lord Jesus, who said every one would hear his voice one day and would be resurrected. The just shall be in the first resurrection at the beginning of the millennium, while the unjust shall be resurrected at the end of the millennium. The reason for the saints to receive glorified bodies at the beginning of the millennium is to live for the thousand years as kings and priests of the most high God.

1 Thessalonians 4:13 But I would not have you to be ignorant, brethren, concerning them which are asleep, that ye sorrow not, even as others which have no hope. 14 For if we believe that Jesus died and rose again, even so them also which sleep in Jesus will God bring with him. 15 For this we say unto you by the word of the Lord, that we which are alive and remain unto the coming of the Lord shall not prevent them which are asleep. 16 For the Lord himself shall descend from heaven with a shout, with the voice of the archangel, and with the trump of God: and the dead in Christ shall rise first: 17 Then we which are alive and remain shall be caught up together with them in the clouds, to meet the Lord in the air: and so shall we ever be with the Lord.

Only those saints who died in Christ will be resurrected at this trumpet call of God. This refers to those saints who will rule the earth for one thousand years as kings and priests, having received glorified bodies. The apostle Paul also confirmed the same words to Timothy, as he taught that only those Christians who suffered shall reign (2 Timothy 2:11-12).

1 Corinthians 15:50 Now this I say, brethren, that flesh and blood cannot inherit the kingdom of God; neither doth corruption inherit incorruption. 51 Behold, I shew you a *mystery; We shall not all sleep, but we shall all be changed, **52** In a moment, in the twinkling of an eye, at the last trump: for the trumpet shall sound, and the dead shall be raised incorruptible, and we shall be changed. **53** For this corruptible must put on incorruption, and this mortal must put on immortality. **54** So when this corruptible shall have put on incorruption, and this mortal shall have put on immortality, then shall be brought to pass the saying that is written, Death is swallowed up in victory.*

Notice carefully in verse 50 that unless a Christian receives a glorified body, he cannot inherit the millennial kingdom of heaven. Therefore when the Lord Jesus returns, it would appear that the only Christians going into the millennium are those with glorified bodies.

Revelation 20:4 *And I saw thrones, and they sat upon them, and judgment was given unto them: and I saw the souls of them that were beheaded for the witness of Jesus, and for the word of God, and which had not worshipped the beast, neither his image, neither had* *received his mark upon their foreheads, or in their hands; and they lived and reigned with Christ a thousand years. 5 But the rest of the dead lived not again until the thousand years were finished. This is the first resurrection.*

We can come to the same understanding and conclusion from these verses as well; if a Christian receives a glorified body he takes part in the first resurrection and enters the millennium. Notice that those who receive a glorified body live and reign with Christ for the millennium. With emphasis upon the reigning, Christians should know that they will rule the world using the word of God as the final authority. The rest of the dead cannot enter the millennium because they do not have glorified bodies. This reference is to Christians who will go to heaven, but will not inherit the millennial kingdom of heaven.

Revelation 2:26 *And he that overcometh, and keepeth my works unto the end, to him will I give power over the nations: 27 And he shall rule them with a rod of iron; as the vessels of a potter shall they be broken to shivers: even as I received of my Father. 28 And I will give him the morning star.*

Kingdom Theology

These verses also teach us that only those Christians that overcome will rule the earth, with a rod of iron which is the word of God. Furthermore, they receive a star which is another word for a glorified body being equal to the angels.

Notes:_____

_____

_____

_____

_____

_____

_____

_____

_____

_____

_____

_____

_____

_____

_____

_____

_____

_____

_____

Kingdom Theology

Second Dispensation of the Kingdom

The second dispensation of the kingdom of heaven and the millennial kingdom
have the same meaning. Before the millennial kingdom begins, the tribulation must end. Let us consider this in these next few verses.

***Revelation 12:7** And there was war in heaven: Michael and his angels fought against the dragon; and the dragon fought and his angels, **8** And prevailed not; neither was their place found any more in heaven. **9** And the great dragon was cast out, that old serpent, called the Devil, and Satan, which deceiveth the whole world: he was cast out into the earth, and his angels were cast out with him. **10** And I heard a loud voice saying in heaven, Now is come salvation, and strength, and the kingdom of our God, and the power of his Christ: for the accuser of our* *brethren is cast down, which accused them before our God day and night. 11 And they overcame him by the blood of the Lamb, and by the word of their testimony; and they loved not their lives unto the death. 12 Therefore rejoice, ye heavens, and ye that dwell in them. Woe to the inhabiters of the earth and of the sea! for the devil is come down unto you, having great wrath, because he knoweth that he hath but a short time. 13 And when the dragon saw that he was cast unto the earth, he persecuted the woman which brought forth the man child. 14 And to the woman were given two wings of a great eagle, that she might fly into the wilderness, into her place, where she is nourished for a time, and times, and half a time, from the face of the serpent.*

Michael the archangel throws the devil out of the first heaven, being the clouds where he has a throne (Isaiah 14:12-14). Notice from verse 10 the words "now", "salvation" and "kingdom". After Satan and his angels are cast down to earth, they know that there remains only three and one-half years until the great tribulation is all over. This is the short time mentioned that the devil has.

"Now" in verse 10 of the scripture is the end of the tribulation. The end of the tribulation is the beginning of the great tribulation. Again, each of these periods is three and one-half years. Perhaps the reason Satan is cast down to the earth for only three and one-half years is because the Lord Jesus ministered for this same amount of time.

Verse 14 states that the woman fled into the wilderness for a time, and times, and a half of time. The word time is interpreted as one year. This is also the three and one-half years of the great tribulation when Satan attacks the woman (church), meaning those foolish virgins who missed the rapture and those who were saved after the rapture took place.

The next two words we should consider from this verse are "salvation" and "kingdom", which happen at the second coming of Christ. At the second coming, those who died in Christ will receive a glorified body. This is known as the first resurrection. We who are alive will be caught up (raptured) and our earthly bodies will become glorified (1 Corinthians 15: 50-54 & 1 Thessalonians 4:13-17). Furthermore, the scripture explains "salvation" in Hebrews

9:28, when the Lord shall appear without sin unto salvation. This is explained as the saving of our bodies, which is also known as the redemption of the purchased possession (Ephesians 1:13-14). This explains why the salvation will take place at the second coming of Christ. Based upon that knowledge, we can safely state that the word "kingdom" here is referring to the millennial kingdom, which begins at the second coming of Christ.

Revelation 20:4 *And I saw thrones, and they sat upon them, and judgment was given unto them: and I saw the souls of them that were beheaded for the witness of Jesus, and for the word of God, and which had not worshipped the beast, neither his image, neither had received his mark upon their foreheads, or in their hands; and they lived and reigned with Christ a thousand years. 5 But the rest of the dead lived not again until the thousand years were finished. This is the first resurrection.*

Once again this dispensation for the next kingdom of heaven is explained here as one thousand years. This millennial kingdom will begin at the second coming of Christ, and will end one thousand years later.

1 Corinthians 15:24 Then cometh the end, when he shall have delivered up the kingdom to God, even the Father; when he shall have put down all rule and all authority and power. 25 For he must reign, till he hath put all enemies under his feet. 26 The last enemy that shall be destroyed is death.

These verses teach when the millennial kingdom will end, and what happens at the end of the millennial kingdom. First, we understand from verse 25 that Christ himself must reign during the millennium. Second, verses 25 and 26 tell us that Christ must put all enemies under his feet, and the last enemy to be destroyed is death. This informs us that death will still be occurring during the millennial reign of Christ, until the end of the millennium, and then it will be thrown into a lake of fire and will reign no more. This information also allows to understand that all nations being unsaved, were not caught up to be at the judgment seat of Christ as were all Christians. But these enter into the millennial kingdom of heaven with mortal bodies and will marry and die during the millennial kingdom of heaven.

Kingdom Theology

Finally, Christ delivers up the kingdom at the end of the millennium. This refers to the third rapture for the church. Christ shall deliver up, meaning rapture, all those new converts who were saved during the millennium, along with those saints having glorified bodies. One reason for this, we are told in Revelation 20, is that the white throne judgment must now take place before we enter the new heaven and new earth.

Notes: _Mother McCalla Furlong_
_No. 11, 2008_

Both.

Third Manifestation of the Kingdom

Revelation 21:1 *And I saw a new heaven and a new earth: for the first heaven and the first earth were passed away; and there was no more sea. **2** And I John saw the holy city, new Jerusalem, coming down from God out of heaven, prepared as a bride adorned for her husband. **3** And I heard a great voice out of heaven saying, Behold, the tabernacle of God is with men, and he will dwell with them, and they shall be his people, and God himself shall be with them, and be their God. **4** And God shall wipe away all tears from their eyes; and there shall be no more death, neither sorrow, nor crying, neither shall there be any more pain: for the former things are passed away. **5** And he that sat upon the throne said, Behold, I make all things new. And he said unto me, Write: for these words are true and faithful. **6** And he said unto me, It is done. I am Alpha and Omega, the beginning and the* *end. I will give unto him that is athirst of the fountain of the water of life freely.* **7** *He that overcometh shall inherit all things; and I will be his God, and he shall be my son.* **8** *But the fearful, and unbelieving, and the abominable, and murderers, and whoremongers, and sorcerers, and idolaters, and all liars, shall have their part in the lake which burneth with fire and brimstone: which is the second death.* **9** *And there came unto me one of the seven angels which had the seven vials full of the seven last plagues, and talked with me, saying, Come hither, I will shew thee the bride, the Lamb's wife.* **10** *And he carried me away in the spirit to a great and high mountain, and shewed me that great city, the holy Jerusalem, descending out of heaven from God,* **11** *Having the glory of God: and her light was like unto a stone most precious, even like a jasper stone, clear as crystal;* **12** *And had a wall great and high, and had twelve gates, and at the gates twelve angels, and names written thereon, which are the names of the twelve tribes of the children of Israel:* **13** *On the east three gates; on the north three gates; on the south three gates; and on the west three gates.* **14** *And the wall* *of the city had twelve foundations, and in them the names of the twelve apostles of the Lamb. 15 And he that talked with me had a golden reed to measure the city, and the gates thereof, and the wall thereof. 16 And the city lieth foursquare, and the length is as large as the breadth: and he measured the city with the reed, twelve thousand furlongs. The length and the breadth and the height of it are equal. 17 And he measured the wall thereof, an hundred and forty and four cubits, according to the measure of a man, that is, of the angel. 18 And the building of the wall of it was of jasper: and the city was pure gold, like unto clear glass. 19 And the foundations of the wall of the city were garnished with all manner of precious stones. The first foundation was jasper; the second, sapphire; the third, a chalcedony; the fourth, an emerald; 20 The fifth, sardonyx; the sixth, sardius; the seventh, chrysolite; the eighth, beryl; the ninth, a topaz; the tenth, a chrysoprasus; the eleventh, a jacinth; the twelfth, an amethyst. 21 And the twelve gates were twelve pearls; every several gate was of one pearl: and the street of the city was pure gold, as it were transparent glass. 22 And I saw no temple therein: for the Lord God Almighty and the Lamb are the temple of it. 23 And the city had no need of the sun, neither of the moon, to shine in it: for the glory of God did lighten it, and the Lamb is the light thereof. 24 And the nations of them which are saved shall walk in the light of it: and the kings of the earth do bring their glory and honour into it. 25 And the gates of it shall not be shut at all by day: for there shall be no night there. 26 And they shall bring the glory and honour of the nations into it. 27 And there shall in no wise enter into it any thing that defileth, neither whatsoever worketh abomination, or maketh a lie: but they which are written in the Lamb's book of life.*

The third manifestation of the kingdom of heaven is explained here as a city, the new Jerusalem. For many thousands of years or more, this city of God (meaning kingdom of heaven) has been in the third heaven. The scriptures are silent on when the third heaven was created and when the kingdom of heaven was created.

Saints who have gone home are allowed to see the outside of the kingdom of heaven but may never be privileged to enter into it. The apostle John opens up our understanding of this kingdom of heaven, and explains the beauty of it. He tells us what it is made up of, he also informs us of the dimensions of this city, and the names listed upon the gates and foundation walls of the city. He calls this city the bride of Christ, and tells us that one day it will leave the third heaven to come down to the earth and remain on the earth for all eternity. Not all Christians dwelling on the earth will be permitted into the kingdom of heaven at this time, for they did not live a godly lifestyle but put themselves first and therefore were denied entrance into this city of God. The glory of God and the throne of Jesus and the father will be in this city. Again we state that many will be denied entrance into this city, because they choose to serve their carnal desires instead of God's desire for their lives.

Revelation 22:14 Blessed are they that do his commandments that they may have right to the tree of life, and may enter in through the gates into the city. 15 For without are dogs, and sorcerers, and whoremongers, and murderers, and idolaters, and whosoever loveth and maketh a lie.

These verses are very difficult to deal with; one reason is the time period. The white throne judgment is over and all devils have been thrown into the lake of fire along with all unsaved mankind. The new heaven and the new earth have started, and the scripture refers to those who enter the city of Jerusalem and those who are left outside. Notice that the kingdom of God is now on the earth after the white throne judgment, and after the new heaven and earth begin.

Although the scripture teaches that all the unsaved are thrown into the lake of fire, we still have those outside of the city of Jerusalem who have practiced the same sins as those thrown into the lake of fire. The real difference between those thrown into the lake of fire and those outside of the city of God after the white throne judgment is that the former group never had their sins forgiven. They never believed that Jesus Christ died for their sins, while the other group outside the city accepted Jesus Christ as their savior.

Although we can speak on this manifestation of the kingdom of heaven, we really cannot speak about the dispensation

Kingdom Theology

with clarity. The reason is that the term "dispensation" means a time with a beginning and an end. Although this last kingdom of heaven has a beginning in the new heaven and new earth, it appears there is no end. This dispensation will continue throughout eternity.

Notes:_____

_____
_____
_____
_____
_____
_____
_____
_____
_____
_____
_____
_____
_____
_____
_____
_____
_____
_____

Kingdom Theology

Entry into the Kingdom Permitted or Denied

The conditions of entering or being denied entry into the kingdom of heaven apply to all three dispensations of the kingdom.

Someone would be denied entry into the first dispensation of the kingdom of heaven because they denied Christ Jesus as their savior. Because of their unbelief concerning Christ's death on the cross for their sin, the scripture states they could not be born again. Some of the disciples were told they would not die until the kingdom of God had come. The condition, however, for entering the kingdom of God was to become born again. The term meant old things would pass away and all things would be made new. It also meant the believer would receive a new heart (spirit) and would become as a little baby inside   (2 Corinthians 5:17). Only those who believed Jesus Christ died for their sins, and rose again on the third day, would become born again (Romans 10:9). The term born again also has other meanings and understandings that apply to it, such as redemption, sanctification, and purification, which all take place when you receive salvation (1 Corinthians 1:30). Once a person is saved, he enters the kingdom of heaven and is a citizen of the kingdom.

The millennial kingdom also has entry conditions. When the millennial kingdom begins, all those who came out of the great tribulation who were not born again will continue to live a normal life. These people do not need a glorified body to enter the millennium, because they will continue to marry, bear children and even die during this period. The condition of entering the millennial kingdom applies only to the Christian. The reason someone would be denied entrance into this kingdom of heaven is because they continued to live a carnal life before they died. Only those saints who overcame, or died in Christ, will be allowed to enter this kingdom of heaven.

Furthermore, at the judgment seat of Christ it will be revealed to these saints who will rule as kings and priests and how many cities they will rule over. The rewards given to these saints will vary from one to five crowns, depending upon their works. In addition, the resurrection will be greater for some than for others, depending on how much they suffered as Christians (Hebrews 11:35).

When the final dispensation of the kingdom of heaven begins, all believers will be back on the earth. Yet not all believers will be allowed entrance into this kingdom of heaven known as the city of God. Some will be denied entrance because of the carnal lives they continued to live before they died. Only those Christians who were found worthy through living godly lives will be allowed entrance into this city of God.

The rewards of entering this kingdom of God are many, for the thrones of Christ and the Father are inside of this kingdom of heaven. The scriptures indicate the half is not told concerning the beauty and splendor inside this kingdom of heaven.

Truly, only those Christians who suffered will be glorified, meaning they will be given glorified bodies. The apostle Paul taught that flesh and blood cannot enter the kingdom of heaven, referring to both the millennial

Kingdom Theology

kingdom and the city of Jerusalem. Only those with glorified bodies will gain entrance into this city of God. This means that the other Christians outside of the city of God were resurrected with mortal bodies, for they cannot get inside of the city (Revelation 22:15, 1 Corinthians 15:50, 2 Corinthians 5:1-4, Revelation 16:16).

Notes:_____

_____
_____
_____
_____
_____
_____
_____
_____
_____
_____
_____
_____
_____
_____
_____
_____
_____

Kingdom Theology

Entry into the Second and Third Kingdoms

The scripture teaches that every born-again believer is in the kingdom of heaven today. We did not come into this kingdom of heaven by keeping commandments but by faith in the death, burial and resurrection of Jesus Christ. Since we did not enter this kingdom of heaven by works, we will never be cast out of this kingdom of heaven because of rebellious deeds of any kind. However, the same theology does not apply concerning the next two kingdoms of God. With this in mind, let us turn to the scriptures for clarity.

Matthew 7:21 Not every one that saith unto me, Lord, Lord, shall enter into the kingdom of heaven; but he that doeth the will of my Father which is in heaven. 22 Many will say to me in that day, Lord, Lord, have we not prophesied in thy name? and in thy name have cast out devils? and in thy name done many wonderful works? 23 And then will I profess unto them, I never knew you: depart from me, ye that work iniquity.

Beloved, this warning of denial is applied to those who work iniquity. Those who are born again, and are already in the first kingdom of heaven, should take to heart the seriousness of being denied entry into the next kingdom of heaven, known as the millennial kingdom. Entering the kingdom of heaven is not based on the power that an individual may have to do miracles. Rather it has to do with the integrity of the individual, living according to the gospel. This is seen in the fruit or lifestyle of the believer and his submissiveness to the gospel of Christ, in the keeping of commandments and doctrinal beliefs.

Matthew 8:11 And I say unto you, That many shall come from the east and west, and shall sit down with Abraham, and Isaac, and Jacob, in the kingdom of heaven. 12 But the children of the kingdom shall be cast out into outer darkness: there shall be weeping and gnashing of teeth.

Luke 13:28 There shall be weeping and

*gnashing of teeth, when ye shall see Abraham, and Isaac, and Jacob, and all the prophets, in the kingdom of God, and you yourselves thrust out. **29** And they shall come from the east, and from the west, and from the north, and from the south, and shall sit down in the kingdom of God. **30** And, behold, there are last which shall be first, and there are first which shall be last.*

When Christ Jesus returns, He will bring with him the next kingdom of heaven. Those saints who are alive and remain, and those believers who are already in the kingdom at that period, will be judged at the judgment seat of Christ. All believers will be judged in the day of judgment for their works good or bad (2 Corinthians 5:10 & Romans 14:10). Here is where rewards are given, or talents are taken away (Matthew 16:27, Revelation 22:12, Matthew 25:14-30). The children of the kingdom are all the believers (church or body of Christ) at the judgment seat of Christ. Many children of the kingdom will be denied entrance into the millennial kingdom, where Abraham, Isaac and Jacob will be present.

Matthew 19:1 *And it came to pass, that when*

Jesus had finished these sayings, he departed from Galilee, and came into the coasts of Judaea beyond Jordan; 2 And great multitudes followed him; and he healed them there. 3 The Pharisees also came unto him, tempting him, and saying unto him, Is it lawful for a man to put away his wife for every cause? 4 And he answered and said unto them, Have ye not read, that he which made them at the beginning made them male and female, 5 And said, For this cause shall a man leave father and mother, and shall cleave to his wife: and they twain shall be one flesh? 6 Wherefore they are no more twain, but one flesh. What therefore God hath joined together, let not man put asunder. 7 They say unto him, Why did Moses then command to give a writing of divorcement, and to put her away? 8 He saith unto them, Moses because of the hardness of your hearts suffered you to put away your wives: but from the beginning it was not so. 9 And I say unto you, Whosoever shall put away his wife, except it be for fornication, and shall marry another, committeth adultery: and whoso marrieth her which is put away doth commit adultery. 10 His disciples say unto him, If the case of the man be so with his wife, it is not good to marry. 11 But he said unto them, All men cannot receive this saying, save they to whom it is given. 12 For there are some eunuchs, which were so born from their mother's womb: and there are some eunuchs, which were made eunuchs of men: and there be eunuchs, which have made themselves eunuchs for the kingdom of heaven's sake. He that is able to receive it, let him receive it.

The teaching on becoming a eunuch is given only to those who are divorced as adulterers. If people divorced as adulterers desire to make it into the millennial kingdom of heaven they would have to become eunuchs. Otherwise, they would be denied entrance into this kingdom (Matthew 19:12).

Matthew 25:14 For the kingdom of heaven is as a man travelling into a far country, who called his own servants, and delivered unto them his goods. 15 And unto one he gave five talents, to another two, and to another one; to every man according to his several ability; and straightway took his journey. 16 Then he that had received the five talents went and traded with the same, and made them other five talents. **17** *And likewise he that had received two, he also gained other two.* **18** *But he that had received one went and digged in the earth, and hid his lord's money.* **19** *After a long time the lord of those servants cometh, and reckoneth with them.* **20** *And so he that had received five talents came and brought other five talents, saying, Lord, thou deliveredst unto me five talents: behold, I have gained beside them five talents more.* **21** *His lord said unto him, Well done, thou good and faithful servant: thou hast been faithful over a few things, I will make thee ruler over many things: enter thou into the joy of thy lord.* **22** *He also that had received two talents came and said, Lord, thou deliveredst unto me two talents: behold, I have gained two other talents beside them.* **23** *His lord said unto him, Well done, good and faithful servant; thou hast been faithful over a few things, I will make thee ruler over many things: enter thou into the joy of thy lord.* **24** *Then he which had received the one talent came and said, Lord, I knew thee that thou art an hard man, reaping where thou hast not sown, and gathering where thou hast not strawed:* **25** *And I was afraid, and went and* *hid thy talent in the earth: lo, there thou hast that is thine.* **26** *His lord answered and said unto him, Thou wicked and slothful servant, thou knewest that I reap where I sowed not, and gather where I have not strawed:* **27** *Thou oughtest therefore to have put my money to the exchangers, and then at my coming I should have received mine own with usury.* **28** *Take therefore the talent from him, and give it unto him which hath ten talents.* **29** *For unto every one that hath shall be given, and he shall have abundance: but from him that hath not shall be taken away even that which he hath.* **30** *And cast ye the unprofitable servant into outer darkness: there shall be weeping and gnashing of teeth.*

This parable is about the kingdom of heaven, or the church. In this parable, the Lord speaks of three individuals who all received talents, a sum of money. All three servants called Jesus Lord when addressing him. The scripture teaches that if any man calls Jesus Lord, he is saved or born again (Romans 10:9). Therefore all three servants were in the first kingdom of heaven.

The first two servants used their talents to

earn more talents, and both heard the same message. These two servants were found worthy to enter the next kingdom of heaven, the millennial kingdom. This is referred to here as the joy of the Lord. The Lord also gives clarity to this interpretation of the joy of the Lord, by rewarding the servants with rule over cities. The first time Christians will rule the earth is during the millennium as kings and priests (Revelation 2:26-28, Revelation 20:4).

The servant that buried his talent, however, heard a different judgment. The word informs us that he was afraid, so he buried his talent, and as a consequence was denied entrance into the joy of the Lord. This servant never learned that perfect love casts out fear, nor did he consider that it was better to fear God than man. Many Christians today refuse to witness for the Lord Jesus, because of fear of losing family, friends, a job, a marriage or many other things.

Luke 9:61 And another also said, Lord, I will follow thee; but let me first go bid them farewell, which are at home at my house. 62 And Jesus said unto him, No man, having put his hand to the plough, and looking back, is fit for the kingdom of God.

The people who are not fit for the kingdom of God are those who start working for God and turn back unto sin. Those people who should be working out their own salvation with fear and trembling have ceased their labors and have gone back to living for themselves, or some other pleasures have drawn them away. Therefore, the scripture states, they are not fit for the kingdom of heaven.

1 Corinthians 6:9 Know ye not that the unrighteous shall not inherit the kingdom of God? Be not deceived: neither fornicators, nor idolaters, nor adulterers, nor effeminate, nor abusers of themselves with mankind, 10 Nor thieves, nor covetous, nor drunkards, nor revilers, nor extortioners, shall inherit the kingdom of God.

The unrighteous spoken of here by the apostle Paul are the born again believers who are living a backsliding life. He mentions fornicators (those having sexual relations with someone other than a spouse), idolaters (those who pray to dead images), and adulterers (spouses who are not faithful). Also the apostle mentions the effeminate, meaning homosexuals and lesbians. The apostle says that those stealing, coveting or lusting after others possessions, drunkards, revilers, and extortioners likewise shall not inherit the kingdom of God. This warning concerns Christians who continue to practice these acts of the flesh rather than those who used to live a selfish lifestyle but have now repented, or those who fell into immorality and then repented again.

Galatians 4:29 But as then he that was born after the flesh persecuted him that was born after the Spirit, even so it is now. 30 Nevertheless what saith the scripture? Cast out the bondwoman and her son: for the son of the bondwoman shall not be heir with the son of the freewoman. 31 So then, brethren, we are not children of the bondwoman, but of the free.

These verses conclude with the allegoric revelation of the apostle Paul concerning Abraham, Sarah, Hagar, Ishmael, and Isaac.

Hagar represents the Old Testament, Sarah is the New Testament. Abraham represents God, and the two children represent the two children of God. Hagar's son Ishmael represents the Jews, while Sarah's son Isaac is representative of Christians. The apostle says that if we as Christians (having Sarah as our mother) go back to obeying the Old Testament (making Hagar our mother) we are to be cast out. The story from Genesis 21 tells us that Sarah told Abraham to cast out Hagar and her son. This is what happens to those Christians who go back under the Mosaic Law; they will be cast out of the millennial kingdom.

Galatians 5:16 This I say then, Walk in the Spirit, and ye shall not fulfil the lust of the flesh. 17 For the flesh lusteth against the Spirit, and the Spirit against the flesh: and these are contrary the one to the other: so that ye cannot do the things that ye would. 18 But if ye be led of the Spirit, ye are not under the law. 19 Now the works of the flesh are manifest, which are these; Adultery, fornication, uncleanness, lasciviousness, 20 Idolatry, witchcraft, hatred, variance,

emulations, wrath, strife, seditions, heresies,
21 *Envyings, murders, drunkenness,*
revellings, and such like: of the which I tell
you before, as I have also told you in time
past, that they which do such things shall not
inherit the kingdom of God.

The apostle Paul wrote to believers, those
who were already in the kingdom of heaven
according to his gospel. When Christians
walk in the flesh, meaning when they go back
to living carnally, they will be denied
entrance into the millennial kingdom. These
acts of the flesh are what will keep Christians
from their inheritance.

One of the things listed here is unlike the
others in verse 20, and that is the word
heresy. This word means a wrong doctrine,
which could also be a doctrine of devils or
seducing spirits. It is hard to imagine that so
many people who are saved are caught up in
cultish doctrines today. This warning of not
inheriting the kingdom of heaven because of
heresy should cause trembling in the church.

Ephesians 5:3 *But fornication, and all*
uncleanness, or covetousness, let it not be
once named among you, as becometh saints;

4 Neither filthiness, nor foolish talking, nor jesting, which are not convenient: but rather giving of thanks. 5 For this ye know, that no whoremonger, nor unclean person, nor covetous man, who is an idolater, hath any inheritance in the kingdom of Christ and of God.

The apostle affirms his warnings to those who are already in the kingdom of heaven, that they will not be found worthy of inheriting the next kingdom of heaven if they are living in the flesh. The millennial kingdom spoken of here is also called the kingdom of Christ and of God.

Hebrews 3:15 While it is said, To day if ye will hear his voice, harden not your hearts, as in the provocation. 16 For some, when they had heard, did provoke: howbeit not all that came out of Egypt by Moses. 17 But with whom was he grieved forty years? was it not with them that had sinned, whose carcases fell in the wilderness? 18 And to whom sware he that they should not enter into his rest, but to them that believed not? 19 So we see that they could not enter in because of unbelief.

Kingdom Theology

This story is about Israel coming out of the land of Egypt and wandering for forty years, until Joshua brought them into the promised land. The apostle reminds us that what happened to those Jews in the physical world still happens to Christians today. These men had provoked the Lord to jealousy with their fornication and worshipping of statues. Therefore they could not enter into the rest of the Lord, or the promised land.

The rest of the Lord spoken of to Christians is the one thousand year kingdom of Christ. In six days God created the earth and rested on the seventh. According to Peter, each day represents a thousand years and this is the timetable we will use to look at the parallel truth. Therefore, six days are six thousand years in the spiritual meaning, and the seventh day is represented by the millennium. At the end of six thousand years, Christ will set up a thousand year kingdom of heaven, known as our rest. Notice, the apostle reminds us, that some Jews did not enter into their physical rest of the promised land, and some Christians may not enter into the spiritual rest of the millennial kingdom. What will keep Christians out of the next kingdom of heaven is a carnal lifestyle rather than a life of faith.

The saints that return for the millennium receive glorified bodies and rule on the earth as kings and priests during the millennial kingdom. All the people saved during the millennial kingdom will have an opportunity to enter into the New Jerusalem if they have been faithful and met the requirements that those saints fulfilled before the millennium started. Although there is not much written about the conditions applying to the saints that were saved during the millennium, I believe the same requirements will be placed upon them as upon us today. The brethren before the millennial kingdom were given certain conditions to fulfill in order to enter into the millennial kingdom.

Once the millennium is over, and the white throne judgment is past, the next dispensation that appears is the new heaven and the new earth. This is the last dispensation to appear according to scripture, and the city Jerusalem which today is in the third heaven will be moved to the earth. This city described in Revelation 21 with all of its glory, and with the thrones of the Father and the Son, will come down to earth. The new heaven and the new earth will receive a new city, which the saints who served the Lord God will be privileged to enter.

Only those saints who receive a glorified body will enjoy entering this city, which has the tree of life in the garden of Eden. This tree of life bears twelve types of fruit which will be eaten by those who have the right to go into the city.

Those saints who enter the city will have no more tears, neither shall the heat of the sun light on them nor the light of the moon. This means that they shall not endure any more sufferings, or testing or trials. These saints shall have the privilege of walking on streets of gold, transparent as glass.

This scripture is meant for all those who overcame, or who laid down their lives for the gospel as martyrs. Those who forsake their lives will earn life with the Lord in his kingdom.

Revelation 22:14 Blessed are they that do his commandments, that they may have right to the tree of life, and may enter in through the gates into the city. 15 For without are dogs, and sorcerers, and whoremongers, and murderers, and idolaters, and whosoever loveth and maketh a lie.

Once the last manifestation of the kingdom of heaven appears on earth, the word of God makes an awesome statement. In verse 14, the blessing is proclaimed concerning those who do the commandments of Christ Jesus. They will have the right to enter the city of God and partake of the tree of life. However, in verse 15 we understand something entirely different about those who are denied entrance into the city. In order to better comprehend this statement, we must consider the things that have already happened.

The millennium has ended, and the white throne judgment is passed. Therefore all those who were in hell have been judged and thrown into the lake of fire. They are no longer in hell, for hell itself is also thrown into the lake of fire. When the new heaven and the new earth come, the city of God, the New Jerusalem, will come down out of the third heaven.

This question must be asked about verse 15, concerning all those people on the outside of the city of God. Since the devils and those who went to hell are in the lake of fire, who are those on the earth outside of the kingdom of heaven? The scripture calls them dogs, and sorcerers, and whoremongers, and idolaters, and whosoever loveth and maketh a lie. Yet these outside of the city are not among those who were in hell or cast into the lake of fire. Why?

The only explanation I can give about these people outside of the kingdom of heaven is that they are believers who lived contrary to the gospel. Although they accepted Jesus Christ as their savior, they lived in pleasure during their earthly lives. These believers did not pay heed to the message of the cross, to deny themselves, nor did they heed the gospel of holiness, to live godly lives. They lived carnally in those sins which are listed as outside of the kingdom of heaven.

Many preachers today believe that when a Christian sins he will lose his salvation and go to hell. Yet the scripture teaches everywhere that the Christian who dies in his sin will not inherit the kingdom of heaven. There is no mention of going to hell or the lake of fire, rather his inheritance of the kingdom of heaven is lost.

Kingdom Theology

Revelation 22:18 *For I testify unto every man that heareth the words of the prophecy of this book, If any man shall add unto these things, God shall add unto him the plagues that are written in this book:* ***19*** *And if any man shall take away from the words of the book of this prophecy, God shall take away his part out of the book of life, and out of the holy city, and from the things which are written in this book.*

The curses in these two verses of scripture are very terrible indeed. In verse 18, Christians can receive the plagues of Egypt, or other plagues, for adding to God's word. Therefore we should consider the gospel that we preach as ministers, and be very careful not to add anything to the scriptures. Similarly, in verse 19, if we take away words, God will take away from Christians our place in the book of life. We may not receive a glorified body, although it is already prepared for us as believers, and the New Jerusalem will also be taken away from us. We will find ourselves outside of the city, fulfilling Revelation 22:15.

Kingdom Theology

Email   address:
wordpowerministry@yahoo.com

Please forward all Bible questions to Apostle Lyle Lee. I will be more than happy to respond to you, beloved.

Dr. Lyle Lee is available for:

Crusades
Revivals
Evangelism
Conventions
Seminars
Teaching

Kingdom Theology

Books; CD's or DVD's

Contact us for our CD ministry or audio tape ministry. We can E-mail to you a complete list of hundreds of topics including metaphors, literal translation, shadows and typologies, genealogy, eschatology, kingdom theology and so on.

We carry a wide range of studies to help those in ministry, or brethren seeking to grow in grace and in the knowledge of the most high.

We also have a book ministry on various subjects for your edification.

We also have a CD ministry or tape ministry on many various subjects for your edification.

We also have some DVD's available on various subjects, each one is filled with a half hour   of   teaching.

Kingdom Theology

Kingdom Theology

Printed in the United States
127836LV00001B/5/P